HOW TO
SEE LIFE
A GUIDE IN

3 2 1

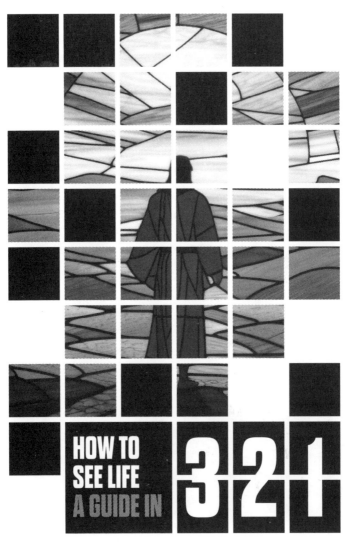

HOW TO SEE LIFE
A GUIDE IN 3 2 1

Glen Scrivener

Publishing
a division of 10ofthose.com

British Library Cataloguing in Publication Data
A record for this book is available from the British Library

ISBN: 9781915705495

Cover design by Sparks Studio

Printed in Denmark

10Publishing, a division of 10ofthose.com
Unit C, Tomlinson Road, Leyland, PR25 2DY, England

Email: info@10ofthose.com
Website: www.10ofthose.com

1 3 5 7 10 8 6 4 2

THIS IS FOR YOU.

CONTENTS

321

INTRODUCTION

AND THEN IT DAWNED ON ME...

4am.

It can't be.

Why is my alarm sounding off at...? A memory surfaces like a shipwreck through the silt: Ack, the video!

A day earlier I had decided to film at the beach—a time-lapse of the sunrise for my next YouTube video. They say the benefit of wise planning is that 'your future self will thank you'.

My future self never thanks me. In fact my present self is often cursing my former self: 'What were you thinking?'

This became my muttered mantra as I pulled on my clothes, noticing already how bright the sky was becoming. 'Smart move, Glen. Filming a sunrise in the summer!'

I drove to a nearby beach and set up the tripod. My camera's time-lapse feature was broken so I was going to have to take a shot manually every 10 seconds then edit them together afterwards: 25 frames per one second of film. In the end I'd get about eight seconds of footage. Oh well, at least it wasn't too cold and the sky was clear, warming gradually into a dappled wash of pinks and oranges. After a while it almost seemed worth it. Until, that is, the event. The nuclear event. Or the alien invasion. Or...

Whatever it was, the intruder made its slow, relentless incursion over the horizon. It emerged as an enormous sliver of piercing light pressing itself up out of the sea—completely out of shot. My camera was pointed 30 degrees too far east. I looked up from the viewfinder where everything was muted: the grey-blue of the ocean, the yellow wisps of cloud, the pink sky. But to the right of my beautifully framed sunrise: there it was—a blaze of iridescent gold, slicing through the pastels of this seaside idyll. And what I'm about to confess to you is one of the most embarrassing admissions of my life. Can you keep a secret? OK, here goes. For three and a half seconds my thoughts were consumed by this one question, *What IS that??*

The one thing it *couldn't* be was the sun. I knew for certain it wasn't the sun, because the sun was due to rise right in the middle of my perfectly framed shot. I'd got up at 4, remember? And the night before I'd consulted an app which I'd downloaded specially for the filming. It assured me of the angle of sunrise. I'd done my homework and I knew precisely where to point my camera. I'm not an idiot, right?

Right?

And so for three and a half seconds my mind gets to work rationalising the situation. Because, the one thing I *know* is that the sun will rise in the middle of my camera's cross-hairs. For the best part of an hour, I'd been fixed on this particular shot: click, wait, click, wait, click, wait. This little plus sign in the centre of my viewfinder, *this* is where the sun goes. *This* is its place. So whatever *that* thing is, over there, out of shot, that must be… what? A ship? An explosion? A… *second* su…?? Aw c'mon. It's not, is it? It can't be.

It is though, isn't it?

It was. It was the sun. Exploding with the equivalent of 10 billion hydrogen bombs per second. Lighting up the sky like a million-watt lamp. The sun was rising in its unmistakably glory. And yet I did mistake it. For some, admittedly brief, portion of my life, I looked at the sun— *the sun*—and refused to acknowledge it for what it was. It did not fit the frame I'd prepared for it and so I lived with a ridiculous contradiction, tying myself in knots before it finally dawned on me in the deepest sense.

I had made an embarrassing mistake. I'd been looking at things all wrong. I had committed to a certain frame and, once I realised, I needed to adjust, to turn, to reframe, to centre myself again on the reason for my being there. I jerked the camera around to capture the last two thirds of the sun's regal ascent from the sea. The time-lapse was ruined. I'd have to do it all again tomorrow—this time with the sun at the centre.

A day later I got the shot I needed (though not the sleep!). My future self did not thank me. But at least he saw the funny side.

REFRAMING

How to See Life: A Guide in 321 is about reframing. It's about changing perspectives in order to look at life again. I think all of us need to do this, no matter our background, no matter our religious affiliations or lack of them. We *all* need to shift perspective. Because—here's an unflattering thought—I reckon you, like me, can focus on all the wrong things. I doubt you're as ridiculous as I was on the beach that morning, but I wonder if you too get distracted, and whether your life is as centred as it could be—or should be.

We all get things wrong. We all fill our vision, at least some of the time, with stuff that's unworthy of our attention. Therefore we need help to refocus on what's important—to reframe our lives and to see things in their proper perspective.

Here's my goal: I want to cast a vision for life that centres on *Jesus*. I happen to believe that Jesus is like the sun and that we are like foolish film-makers, focusing on all the wrong things. You might not share that belief (yet), but in the interests of full disclosure I feel I should declare my biases. I'm a Jesus-guy and I want to show you what life looks like when you put *him* in the cross-hairs of your viewfinder.

THE PLAN

The plan for *How to See Life: A Guide in 321* is simple. Whether you've been a Christian for decades or whether you've never considered the faith, I want to do a couple of things. First, I want to show you Jesus, *then* I want to show you life *as illuminated by Jesus*. Both those things are necessary. Because if Jesus is like the sun, then you can look at the sun (if you're careful!). But you can also look at everything else by the light of the sun. That's the plan.

We begin in the first section by examining the story of Jesus. At points we'll be using the Gospel of John (that's the fourth biography of Jesus in the Bible, written by his close companion called John). As John introduces Jesus he says:

> *In him was life, and that life was the light of all mankind. The light shines in the darkness, and the darkness has not overcome it.* **JOHN 1:4–5**

Jesus' arrival in history is like the sunrise…

> *The true light that gives light to everyone was coming into the world.* **JOHN 1:9**

And when Jesus proclaims his own identity, he declares:

> *I am the Light of the world. Whoever follows me will never walk in darkness but will have the light of life.* **JOHN 8:12**

There is a brilliance to Jesus that has attracted billions down through the ages. Many have found in him something irresistible—something that has caused them to reframe their lives. History itself has turned on the coming of

Christ and our modern vision of life has been shaped by Jesus more than any other figure.

Whether you call yourself a Christian or not, the way you see life, love, beauty, truth, goodness, meaning, purpose, and destiny will owe more to Jesus than anyone else. That's because Christianity has been the world's most enduring and influential view of life. In the history of the world, more people have oriented their lives to *Jesus* than to any other focal point. At his arrival, history turned. The clocks were reset. The world has never been the same.

Therefore as we look at the story of Jesus, we're encountering something that really has illuminated life. Jesus has, in fact, been like a dawning light to this world.

And once we've looked at Jesus, we're in a position to look at life *in the light of* Jesus (that's the middle three sections). In particular we will explore Jesus' vision for God, the world, and ourselves. According to Jesus, life is all about God's THREE-ness, the world's TWO-ness and our ONE-ness. Don't worry about the numbers right now, they'll be explained as we go.

From the contents page you'll see the final section is a selection of FAQs (Frequently Asked Questions) which turn to common critiques of Christianity. You may consider some or all of these questions to be barriers to Christian faith. You may think there should be another dozen besides. You're right. There could be another six dozen!

But I hope it's OK if we address these 12, and to do so at the end. I tend to think that questions are best asked and answered once we've got our bearings. On the beach that morning I had three and a half seconds of the most urgent questions. But my questions were the wrong questions, asked from the wrong perspective. Once I'd reframed things, I saw the questions (and the answers—*and myself!*) in a new light.

It's like that with Christian faith. I had many questions before I'd become a Christian. Many of those questions have changed now, and so have I. But I still have questions— far more than before. Faith in Jesus hasn't erased my doubts but it has re-oriented the way I view them. In so many ways the invitation to Christian faith is an invitation to *embrace* certain questions, not to eradicate them. What's more, it causes us to *ask* questions of ourselves and of the beliefs we once held dear. With Jesus we end up with more questions, and that's OK. The goal is not so much to solve all problems, but to frame them properly.

Having said all that, if you feel you have to skip ahead to the FAQs, by all means take a sneak peek. But I think if you wait, you'll get a more rounded view of how these issues fit into the whole.

GETTING THE MOST OUT OF THE BOOK

Here are three ways you can get the most out of *How to See Life: A Guide in 321*. (Explore your options at 321course.com)

READ

JOHN'S GOSPEL.

 I've put together a guide which you can access on Bible.com and on YouVersion, the world's biggest Bible app. In 21 five-minute readings you'll be introduced to history's greatest figure via the world's all-time bestseller! Each reading includes a brief thought and some questions for reflection. There is a shining brilliance to Jesus in the Bible. I can only describe it second-hand. I urge you to see him for yourself.

EXPERIENCE

321—THE ACCOMPANYING COURSE.

 Alongside this book there's a course you won't want to miss. *321* can be viewed online or on your mobile device right now. The course is personalised, so you'll need to create an account with your email and a password to access the content. Don't worry, it only takes a few seconds to set up, and it's completely free. Watch the gorgeous animations, bringing

each chapter's story to life, and enjoy the multi-media experience. Why not take your time to both read and then watch the content, soaking it in and giving yourself space to think it all through.

JOIN

WITH OTHERS.

 I've helped tens of thousands of people to 'see life' according to *321* and whenever I do it in groups, I always learn something new. We see more when we're all looking *together*. So why not experience the course or read the book with a friend, or a bunch of friends? Find ways of connecting with others, online or in person.

Enough of the introduction. Let's get to it. It's time to meet the star of the show…

321

JESUS: OUR GUIDE

CHAPTER 1

LOST IN SPACE

WHAT GETS YOU THINKING?

We rarely take the time in our busy lives, but occasionally something grabs our attention and makes us question the meaning of it all. It might be the beauty of the world or the tragedy of life. It could be the joys of a newborn child or the sorrow of losing a loved one—what makes you ask the big questions about life, meaning and purpose?

PICTURE THIS:

A WOMAN WAKES UP ON A SPACE STATION WITH NO MEMORY OF HOW SHE GOT THERE

She sits up, then regrets it. Her vision blurs, head swims and a battle ensues between the nausea rising and the air she's gulping down.

Her gasps echo down the corridor.

There's a clatter and then approaching footsteps. As she grips the side of her bed, she realises it's more of a capsule. A pod. A... *what?*

Blinking away her tears, a man comes into view.

'Well I'll be,' he says. 'You're up.'

The word 'up' bounces around the daze with nowhere to land. If this is 'up', where is 'down'? Where is anything?

Some more footsteps draw near and she hears a female voice. 'Is she awake? I knew it. I knew she'd come to.'

Getting control over her nausea, she pants three times, blows out her cheeks and tries swinging her legs over the side. Another headrush.

'Whoa there,' says the man.

Hunched and out of breath she croaks her first word, 'Water.'

The man grabs a flask while the woman rubs her back. 'I'm Hope,' says the woman.

As she sips, she looks to the man.

'Doc,' he says.

Lowering the flask, she gapes like an actor waiting to be fed her line. Hope obliges.

'Your tag says Sasha.'

Sasha closes her mouth. She hoped for recognition but the name feels as alien as everything else.

Hope smiles. 'I didn't feel like a Hope either. But what do *we* know?'

Sasha stares across the room. There are two other pods, both vacant, a table with three chairs, and, on the far side, a large window. Slowly the stars are turning. Or is it the ship? After a moment she blinks hard, returning her focus to the others.

'Good question,' says Sasha.

'What question?'

'What *do* we know?'

If this were a scene from a movie, what kind of movie would it be? Science fiction, certainly. But more particularly it feels, at this point, like a science fiction *horror*. There are mysterious—possibly malevolent—forces at work. No one really knows what's going on. The doors are locked and no one is getting out alive. It's certainly not a pleasant set-up for a story. No one wants to be in Sasha's shoes. And yet—I want to suggest—you *are* in Sasha's shoes. You are, in fact, Sasha. Or you're Doc. Or you're Hope.

Really? Yes, kind of. A bit.

We're all thrown into this world with profound questions: Who are we? How did we get here? What is the meaning of this? Is anything out there? Anything beyond? Any help?

And if there's no help, perhaps we're just stuck in this thing as, one-by-one, we're picked off…

As we wrestle with this predicament, each of us take different views.

Some of us are more like Hope. There she is on the space station, sitting for long hours at the window, gazing out at the stars in awe. The beauty feeds her. She sees purpose in all that's happening. She can't tell you why but... she's hopeful.

Some of us are like Doc. He's a scientist. You could imagine him trying to make sense of the situation. He starts observing the design of the ship, the well-tuned mechanics of it all, the perfectly timed provisions that allow them to live day-by-day. Everything is just right. It all seems eerily set up for them.

'It stands to reason,' he says, 'they're actually providing for us. Someone wants us here.'

But then, some of us are like Sasha. When Doc says 'Someone wants us here', she can't contain herself.

'And that's a good thing?' she asks. 'Who... *wants* us... here?! And how do you know? How does anyone know?'

That's Sasha. She's not convinced by Doc and his reasoning. She's not convinced by Hope and her optimism. She's just not convinced.

ARE YOU A HOPE, A DOC OR A SASHA?

Some people are like Hope. They sense that there's more going on than can be seen, and maybe they feel like 'Someone up there likes us.' Nowadays they might call themselves spiritual or religious or—most commonly today—'spiritual but not religious'. Actually though, down through history, the great majority of humankind have had a Hope-like view of reality. Before the period we call modernity almost everyone saw the world through spiritual lenses.

Still today, the great majority of people in the world are not atheists. Even for the shrinking percentage of the world's population that identify as atheists (currently about 16% and falling), many still believe in a higher power, or prayer, or the afterlife. They express beliefs in 'something more'. Hope seems to represent the majority view of humans thrust into this dangerous world.

But there are also Docs. The Docs of this world study their environment: logically, scientifically, mathematically. And many of them conclude that we live in a world fine-tuned for life—fine-tuned for *us*. So they reason, 'If there's design, there's a Designer, if there's architecture, there's an Architect.' They can't tell you much about such a Creator but for many people their science and reason leads them towards a belief in some kind of God.

That was the view of the first modern scientists. Five hundred years ago, the pioneers of modern science were consciously overturning pre-modern views. They refused to have a purely spiritual worldview, they wanted to investigate and test the world. But doing so did not destroy their faith in God, it confirmed it. They considered the evidence of this world as evidence *for* a Creator, and today many scientists agree (for more see our FAQs).[1]

Others, though, are not convinced.

The Sashas of this world say, 'Well designed? Really? Sure there are some nice parts to life, but there's plenty wrong too. And if we're calling this world "well designed"—well designed compared to what? This universe is the only one we've got. In fact, if there *is* a Grand Architect, maybe he's a sadist. We just don't know.'

All these kinds of people exist today and, quite honestly, I can flit between each of these views several times before breakfast. We make sense of the world via our sixth sense, or our science, or our scepticism, or—most often—by some combination of the three. But usually we have a preference. If you were on that space station, who would you be?

---

1 I'm not asking you to share Doc's view. I'm just pointing out that there *are* Docs in the world today. It's true that some people think of science as ruling out the need for faith. But others think that science points us *towards* faith. You can read more about faith and science in the FAQs.

THE TWIST

Before you answer, I have to tell you the story is not over. Hope, Doc and Sasha spend weeks on board arguing about the meaning of it all, but one day changes everything.

Like a car crash, they feel it before they hear it, and they hear it before they see it.

The ground lurches beneath their feet, throwing Hope to the floor. Doc stumbles into Sasha.

'Get off!'

'Airlock engaged,' reports the online computer.

Sasha looks fiercely at Doc. 'What airlock?'

'Nothing to do with me,' he says, placing a steadying hand on the wall. 'Maybe instead of arguing we should have been on the lookout.'

'Lookout? Why should we be looking out? What exactly are we looking to...'

'Guys!' Hope interrupts, still prostrate on the floor. 'Look.'

Above a door at the far end of the corridor, five lights begin to flick in sequence from red to green. All eyes fix on the fifth as, with a long beep, it switches.

There is a thud and a violent hiss as the door opens, heavy and slow.

Hope, Doc and Sasha can do nothing but watch as a stranger steps over the threshold. He walks cautiously, eager not to frighten the three. He pauses to remove his helmet and Sasha is surprised to find a human face staring back at her. Then she's surprised at her surprise. *Of course he's human, what else would he be?*

But that's just it. He could be anything. Given this space station, given their plight, all bets are off.

Sasha finds herself inching towards the man. They all do. And it begins to feel as though their collective bafflement fixes to this stranger like iron filings to an electromagnet. All their questions are now questions for *him*.

'How?' Doc whispers.

'Long story,' says the stranger.

'Where have you come from?' asks Hope.

'Home,' he says.

'Who are you?' Sasha demands.

'I'm the Rescue.'

Let's press pause. Where are we now in the story? With this twist, the plot might still be a horror. The stranger could turn out to be the embodiment of all their deepest fears. But suddenly there's the possibility of a different kind of story—one with a different kind of ending.

The plot has very much taken a turn. The entrance of this stranger changes the conversation on that ship—it changes the story. It has to. Hope, Doc and Sasha had their theories and their many disputes but now they must do business with this man. They cannot ignore him. His arrival is too earth-shattering, the possibilities are too great. They'll have to make their mind up about the stranger.

Maybe they'll all disbelieve him. Maybe they'll conclude that he's come from another part of the ship and he has delusions of grandeur. Maybe they will think they've all got cabin fever and they've dreamt him up. They will definitely want to pepper him with questions: *Who are you really? Where have you come from? Prove it!* But whether they believe him or not, his arrival is *the* plot twist in their story. All their other questions find a focal point: What to make of this man?

WHO IS HE?

And of course, Jesus is that man. Jesus is the man who has come into the middle of our world—the middle of history—splitting it in two. Every year prior to his birth is counted as a year *before* him. Every year afterwards has been counted as a year *since* him. At the centre of the human story stands a man who makes extraordinary claims.

Some religious figures claim they've heard messages from beyond this world. Jesus says he has come from beyond. He isn't just *really sure* about God. He doesn't just hear voices from the other side. He doesn't just bring messages from heaven. He keeps saying he is our Maker and he has come in person, not just to bring a message, but to rescue us—to rescue the *world*—from its estrangement, darkness and death. That's his claim anyway. And that's very different.

What do you make of Jesus?

You could be like Hope, or like Doc, or like Sasha, or any number of different characters. Christians have all sorts of personalities. But whatever your temperament, the big question is: What do you make of *Jesus*? Is he who he says he is? If he is, it changes everything.

WATCH

'LOST IN SPACE'

FOR REFLECTION

- Did the idea of the space station make sense as a picture of life? What stood out to you?

- Who do you relate to most—Hope, Doc or Sasha? Why?

- If you were there, how would you react to the entrance of that fourth person?

CHAPTER 2

THE GREATEST STORY EVER TOLD

WHO IS JESUS?

Jesus' identity has been one of the most hotly contested questions down through history. Different people have considered him a prophet, a guru, a shadowy figure of history, a myth, the Son of God come in the flesh. What about you? How have you formed your view and has it changed over time? What do you think it would be like to meet Jesus?

PICTURE THIS:

A SCREENWRITER PITCHES HER LATEST MOVIE IDEA TO A HOLLYWOOD EXECUTIVE. IT DOESN'T GO WELL

```
FADE IN


INT. BILL'S OFFICE - DAY


JUDY is sitting on a very low couch with
a manuscript on her lap. She looks up
past BILL's expensive shoes resting on
the desk. He's leaning right back in his
chair and playing absent-mindedly with a
toy basketball.
```

                          BILL
           (pointing his index finger at Judy
                     like a gun)
          You have my undivided attention: Go!

                          JUDY
                      (sceptical)
          Okay… Well… Meet Marko Ivanov, a
          Ukrainian car mechanic from a small
          town outside Donetsk.

Bill looks at her.

                     JUDY (CONT'D)
          It's in the Donbas.

Bill is still none the wiser.

                     JUDY (CONT'D)
          A Russian-held region in Ukraine.

                          BILL
         (feet off the desk, leaning forwards)
            OK, so we've got a Rambo on
            our hands. One man against
            an evil empire.

                         JUDY
          Well... kind of but not really.
          He doesn't fight.

                         BILL
          So, like a spy?

Judy looks down at her manuscript, trying
to collect herself.

                         JUDY
          He stays out of the conflict
          altogether. He doesn't join the
          army, or any of the political
          parties, or the Russians. He even
          quits being a car mechanic and
          becomes a travelling speaker.

                         BILL
                    (frowning)
          From grease monkey to
          inspirational influencer?

                         JUDY
          Well. No, but kind of. Look, he
          starts speaking to the people —
          crowds of ordinary people — about
          life. About a life that is far

larger than Ukraine or Russia or war
or anything. And it connects. He
attracts this unlikely following:
powerful women and working men;
sex workers and government
officials; pro-Russian and pro-
Ukrainian activists.

                    BILL
He goes viral all around the world.

                    JUDY
No! Well yes, but
only after he dies.

                    BILL
                (wincing)
After... your inspirational
grease monkey dies... he *then*
becomes famous?

                    JUDY
                 (sighs)
OK, let me level with
you. He's Jesus.

                    BILL
            (taking time to process)

...He's a *delusional* inspirational grease monkey?!

                    JUDY
No, I mean, the car mechanic, Marko,
is Jesus. This is the 21st-century
update of the Jesus story. This
is how the Jesus story would have
happened if it happened today.

                    BILL
               (incredulous)
The Son of God... is a
Ukrainian car mechanic?

                    JUDY
                (relieved)
You get it!

                    BILL
                 (firmly)
I promise you, I do not. What does
our car mechanic do for miracles?
Water into vodka?

                    JUDY
That's actually not a bad idea.

Bill is lost. Judy pushes through undaunted.

                    JUDY (CONT'D)
          I know how it sounds, that's the
          point. I mean, c'mon, this blue
          collar nobody is the Son of God?
          That's dynamite. And he travels
          around nowhere towns, transforming
          lives and causing trouble, until
          the authorities decide they've
          had enough. Soldiers arrest him
          and he's tortured to death. They
          completely crush him in this... this
          excruciating public execution.

Bill is waiting for her to go on.
Judy is finished.

                    BILL
          ...Please tell me that's
          not your ending.

                    JUDY
          Honestly I don't know the ending
          yet. I don't know whether
          21st-century audiences will
          believe, you know...

                          BILL
          ...he resurrected?

                          JUDY
          Yeah.

                          BILL
          You've got the Lord of the Universe
          doing wheel alignments and you're
          worried about believability?

Judy laughs weakly.

                     BILL (CONT'D)
          Judy, I think you're a terrific
          writer, I really do but you're
          wasting your time on this Jesus
          story. Why don't you switch tracks?
          Come work on our latest picture,
          I'll give you an additional
          writing credit.

                          JUDY
                    (sighs, deflated)
          I'll think about it.
          What's the story?

                              BILL
               You'll love it. All about
               an unlikely superhero who
               gives everything to rescue
               the galaxy. We're calling it
               Saviour. Whaddaya say?

        Judy rises to take BILL's hand.

                              JUDY
                       (sarcastically)
               Where do they get their ideas?

                              BILL
                        (genuinely)
               I know, right?

        FADE OUT

A STORY IN TIME —FOR ALL TIME

If you want a modern parallel for the Jesus story, our
Ukrainian car mechanic is a decent approximation. This is
how Jesus would come across if he came in the 21st rather
than 1st century: a blue-collar nobody in a war-torn land.

Jesus was born into poverty and obscurity in a despised part of Israel—a land under the thumb of mighty Rome. He worked as a carpenter for the great majority of his life until, aged 30, he turned into a wandering preacher, touring around nowhere towns and villages. He never went to the right schools, never took religious orders, never entered political life, never joined the military, never founded a school or a dynasty, or even a family. He never wrote a book. He never had an ounce of earthly power or prestige.

But wherever he went miracle stories followed—miracles that demonstrated not only tremendous power but heartfelt compassion. He calmed a storm to save his friends, he fed the hungry, healed the sick, cleansed the lepers, raised the dead. But through it all he was adamant that his mission was not simply to teach or to heal. His mission was to die.

As a young man in his early 30s he endured the most shameful death the Romans could inflict—a death so torturous those seeing his execution would never be tempted to follow in his footsteps. After just three years in the public eye, that should have been that for the Jesus Movement.

But then his followers made the extraordinary claim: the one crucified has risen, never to die again. He had gone through death and come out into unending, unbounded life, peace and joy.

They started preaching this message and the revolution began. This world has never been the same.

There's a reason why people have called this *the greatest story ever told*. It's difficult to imagine a greater one. All our human stories follow one of a few familiar patterns: there's overcoming the monster; rags to riches; the quest; voyage and return; and they all tend to follow the basic shapes of romance, tragedy or comedy.[2] But the Jesus story seems like the OmniStory! Here we have it all: out of love for the world, the King of heaven becomes poor, only to be raised up again to a place of honour. On a quest to save us he comes to earth to overcome the monster—death. He takes on our tragedy to turn it into his comedy and brings about a happily ever after. There's something profoundly mythological about all this. It's like a mash-up of every ancient trope. No wonder 'Bill, the Hollywood Exec' wants to make a superhero movie called *Saviour*. We all resonate with the story of an unlikely hero bringing redemption though sacrifice. It's the story we can't stop telling.

But with Jesus, it's not just mythological. There's also something unavoidably historical here. Read the Gospels and you won't find any undefined 'once upon a times' or 'lands far away'. Jesus showed up in history in a certain time and place. He was born in Bethlehem during the reign of Caesar Augustus, he was sentenced to die by the fifth governor of the province of Judea and was crucified

---

2   See Christopher Brooker, *The Seven Basic Plots* (Continuum, 2004).

under the reign of Caesar Tiberius. His life was lived here, not in Dream Time or Fantasy Land.

While the Jesus story is epic in its proportions, it happens in the ordinariness of history—of *our* history. The OmniStory is earthed into our reality. And if we see these things come together in Jesus we can say: *the stories are true.* There *is* a Hero who redeems through sacrifice, who trades it all for love, who slays the dragon of death, who turns all things to a 'happily ever after'. For Christians, these things are not merely matters of hope, they are matters of history.

And they have *made* history too.

THE ULTIMATE MIRACLE

A penniless preacher, Jesus was slaughtered as a criminal *and since then he has been worshipped by billions.* It's like Marko, the car mechanic, becoming Saviour of the world. Jesus' movement is the largest, most diverse sociological phenomenon the world has ever seen. It's been growing from the first century till now and has transformed the world unimaginably.

Historian Tom Holland says, 'we remain the children of the Christian revolution: the most disruptive, the most influential and the most enduring revolution in history'.[3] And that's extraordinary. You can understand how a

---

3   Tom Holland, *Revolutionary* (SPCK, 2020), p9. For more from Tom Holland you can read his epic history of the West as a history of Christian influence, *Dominion: The Making of the Western Mind* (Little, Brown, 2019).

ruthless general or a great emperor might change the world, but what about Jesus—an ex-builder's labourer, executed in his 30s?

Jesus has fashioned our world in terms of our assumptions and intuitions. The way we view life has been affected by Jesus more than anyone else. He has shaped the way we see God and goodness, humanity and history. In the West, our sense of meaning and morals derive from Jesus more than from any other source. He has made our world.[4]

You may have heard that Jesus turned water into wine. But that's nothing compared to the enduring miracle of Jesus *himself*. Somehow he has turned crucifixion into world domination. That's some miracle.

WHO IS THIS MAN?

The Bible says he's far more than just a man. In John's Gospel, Jesus is 'the Word of God':

> *In the beginning was the Word and the Word was with God and the Word was God. He was with God in the beginning.* **JOHN 1:1–2**

To be 'the Word of God', means that Jesus is the communication of God. God has something to say to the world, and that something is not so much a poem

---

4 For more on this claim, I wrote a whole book elaborating on this paragraph called *The Air We Breathe* (The Good Book Company, 2022). Or you could watch my short documentary, *Easter Uprising*: https://speaklife.org.uk/videos/easter-uprising/

or a principle. It's not a creed or a command. What God wants to say to the world is 'Jesus'. And his message has never changed.

As the eternal Son of God, Jesus has always existed with his Father and the Holy Spirit. That whole idea—'Father, Son and Holy Spirit'—will be covered in the next section. For now, let's just say that Jesus is 100% *in* on what it means to be God. That's why 'Son of God' is a fitting title for Jesus. He's a chip off the old block; just like his Father. When you're looking at Jesus you're seeing God—so says John in the Bible.

Growing up, I never warmed to the idea of God or 'the Church' or institutional religion. All that stuff left me cold. But then, as an adult, I took a proper look at the person of Jesus and that changed everything. I read through the Gospels and was floored by Jesus. I kept thinking, there's no one like him. As I read I came to the conclusion: If *he* is what God is like, I'm in.

I describe myself as a bit like the woman who's always been dead against the institution of marriage. She constantly speaks against this 'traditional construct' called marriage, right until she meets Mr Right. And then she falls for him. And maybe she even marries the guy. Why? Because she loves marriage? No. Because she loves *him*. And he's converted her.

FULL OF GRACE AND TRUTH?

According to the Bible, Jesus didn't just begin a religion. He began the universe.

Through him all things were made... **JOHN 1:3**

A monster claim! But consider: maybe this is what explains the impact of Jesus. Maybe this is why a penniless preacher has 'made our world'—giving us our morals, meaning and vision for life. Maybe he has 'made our world' because he is, in fact, the Maker, entering his world to set it straight:

The Word became flesh and made his dwelling among us. We have seen his glory—the glory of the one and only Son who came from the Father, full of grace and truth. **JOHN 1:14**

This is describing Christmas. The Son of God became flesh. He joined our human family forever, becoming our Brother. And what's he like? He's 'full of grace and truth'. That's an attractive combination. Think of someone full of grace. They're full of compassion and mercy, forgiveness and love. Now think of someone full of truth—they're a real straight shooter, they tell it how it is. Have you got those two people in mind—they're quite different, aren't they? In Jesus these opposites combine.

In chapter 2 of John's Gospel, Jesus goes to a wedding and they're out of wine. No problem—Jesus miraculously turns water into the finest of wines. Most people think God would go to parties to change wine into water. Jesus is different. With him it's water into wine. He's full of grace.

Yet, turn the page in John and the next thing you'll read is how Jesus goes to the temple—the holiest building on the planet. Once there, Jesus sees it full of religious hypocrisy and people making a fast buck. So he weaves a whip together to drive out the livestock on sale. He turns over the tables of these peddlers and con men, scatters their money and forces everyone out. He's full of uncompromising truth.

Think of it: he goes to the party and brings wine; he goes to the temple and brings a whip. Who *is* this guy? A Christian is someone who looks at Jesus and concludes he is more than a man. Jesus is Lord.

JESUS IS LORD

Don't be put off by the religious sounding phrase: 'Jesus is Lord.' Everybody thinks something is Lord, something is Boss—something is ultimately running the show. Some think money makes the world go round. Others think it's power, or maybe it's the iron laws of nature, or chaotic forces, or disparate gods, or a distant deity, or fate. But a Christian says: 'No, over and above the rest, *Jesus* is Lord. He is the controlling reality of life.'

In the rest of the book we'll explore the implications of this one truth.

To say 'Jesus is Lord' means that *Jesus* shows us what **GOD** is like (that's chapters 3 and 4).

To say 'Jesus is Lord' means *Jesus* shows us what the **WORLD** is like (chapters 5 and 6).

To say 'Jesus is Lord' means *Jesus* shows us what **YOU** are like (chapters 7 and 8).

This is why the book is structured around these four sections: Jesus; God; the World; and You. We're considering life according to Jesus. But it all turns on him.

As you read, though, be warned: considering Jesus might seriously disrupt your life. Back when I was 21, I was halfway through reading Luke's Gospel and I just couldn't escape the thought that Jesus is Lord. It was a case of: *All right, you got me! Jesus is it. He's the One!* That's how it happens. It sneaks up on you *and suddenly—bad luck, you're a Christian.*

I'm only half joking about that.

Many of us have become Christians without really meaning to. All we were doing was exploring the Bible or looking into Jesus or hearing about him from a friend or a preacher or a book or a course, and all of a sudden we were gripped. It's discovering a truth that you can't leave at arm's length. It's encountering a person who reorients your whole vision—your whole life. If it hasn't happened to you yet, pray that it does. It's not 'bad luck', really. It's the best of disruptions. With Jesus at the centre of your vision you will encounter a movement and—more importantly—a *God* unlike anything the world can offer.

WATCH

'THE GREATEST STORY EVER TOLD'

FOR REFLECTION

- What have been your views of God in the past?

- What have been your views of Jesus in the past?

- What difference does it make to consider that Jesus is what God is like?

OPTIONAL READING PART I

If you really want to see life according to Jesus, nothing beats a first-hand encounter with our Guide. You can access our special reading plan on Bible.com or the YouVersion app (see the link on p.16). If that's not your style, then here, between the main sections of the book, I suggest an even simpler reading plan—seven chapters at a time. (Don't worry, chapters in the Bible are very short.) I recommend using a modern translation like the NIV which is the translation used in the book. I've also offered some questions for reflection. This is obviously all entirely optional, but I highly recommend 'seeing Jesus' for yourself. I think you'll soon understand why John is the most read piece of literature in the world and why Jesus is history's greatest Figure.

JOHN CHAPTERS 1—7

QUESTIONS FOR REFLECTION:

- 'The Word' is a title for Jesus (John 1:1; 1:14), it means he is the communication or revelation of God: What kind of God does Jesus reveal?

- Jesus comes across some very different characters in these chapters. How does he respond to them?

- How does Jesus speak of himself, his Father and his mission?

- What do you think it would be like to meet Jesus?

GOD'S THREE-NESS

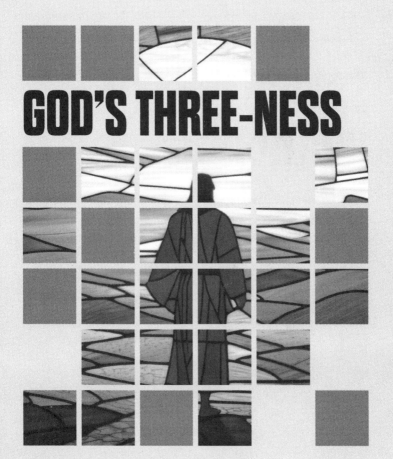

CHAPTER 3

SAVING PRIVATE PHILIPS

WHAT IS YOUR PICTURE OF GOD?

When you hear the word 'God', where does your mind turn? What images spring to mind? Or phrases? Whether you believe in him or not, what are you thinking about when you think about God?

PICTURE THIS:

A SOLDIER IS BLEEDING OUT FROM HIS WOUNDS. HE WHISPERS A FINAL QUESTION WHICH THE CHAPLAIN WILL TAKE A LIFETIME TO ANSWER

Daybreak revealed the scale of the losses.

The night before—17th October 1944—the allies had attempted a surprise attack on the German position. But the northern Italian town of San Martino provided excellent defences for the Germans—high ground and thick walls.

Through the night and into the morning, Tom Torrance had acted as stretcher bearer for the King's Own Royal Rifles. He was their chaplain and known to all as Padre—'Father'. As daylight filtered through he came across one solider he would never forget.

Private Philips was 19 years old and bleeding heavily. It was clear he didn't have long. As the chaplain bent down and leant over him to unbuckle his water bottle, the young man had one question.

'Padre, is God really like Jesus Christ?'

What is God *like*?

It's a question we rarely consider. But sometimes we're jolted from the demands of the present and we ask life's biggest question.

Before that day in northern Italy, Private Philips had believed in God. But he may not have thought much about what God was *like*. 'God' can be an incredibly slippery word. It represents different things to different people. And even if we say the word a lot, that doesn't mean we've thought much about its meaning.

This is true for those who believe in God and for those who don't. Everyone uses the word and we all assume we know *how* it's being used. But do we?

Personally, although I believed in God as a youngster, I thought of God a bit like I thought of electricity. I knew electricity was powerful—I thought of God as powerful. I didn't understand electricity—I didn't understand God. I knew that if you harnessed the power of electricity it could help you—I thought the same about God. And I knew that if you got on the wrong side of electricity then Zap! Ditto God.

I believed in 'God' but, unsurprisingly, I never warmed to the idea of him. Perhaps you don't either.

WHICH GOD DON'T YOU BELIEVE IN?

Let me tell you about another chaplain also called Tom—one who was also asked questions by 19-year-olds. Tom Wright was the chaplain at Worcester College, Oxford between 1986 and 1993. Students would sometimes tell him, 'I don't believe in God' but he was never fazed by this. Instead he would ask a question back: 'Which God is it you don't believe in?'

The student would look a little puzzled but Tom Wright would press them to describe the God they doubted. Usually they would sketch out an unappealing vision: some lonely individual, high on power, low on personality—beard, angry look, thunderbolt ready to hurl. Zeus basically. The chaplain would listen and then say, 'I'm not surprised you don't believe in that God. I don't believe in that God either... I believe in the God I see revealed in Jesus.'

When Tom Wright imagined God, he pictured Jesus. That's a very biblical idea. Jesus is called the image of God (Colossians 1:15) and the exact representation of God (Hebrews 1:3). Multiple times in the Bible he's called the Son of God—he's the spitting image of his Father. This theme saturates John's Gospel.

John's biography explains early on that, 'No one has ever seen God, but [his only Son] has made him known' (John 1:18). We don't know what God is like but Jesus, the Son of God, reveals him. So if we want to know what God is like, we need to ask: What kind of God does *Jesus* reveal?

In so many ways, the Gospels represent the answer to that question. They tell the most compelling story. As we saw in the last chapter: Jesus is born into poverty, lives among the people, works as a carpenter before becoming the most famous teacher and storyteller the world has known. He walks around planet earth like he owns the place, commanding nature, but using all of his powers to save, bless, feed, cleanse and heal. His goal, though, is never to take applause but to give his life. This is what he does on the cross, dying in our place, to take our death and then to rise up again to share his life with us.

This is the central message of Christianity: '*Jesus* is what God is like'. He is God's explanation. Our questions about God find a focus in the person of Jesus. Therefore if we want to know what God is like we need to look closer at this man, this hero, this story. He is literally on his knees serving the weak, the filthy, the poor, the despised. He tells the whole world that he *is* the Image of God and then, with all eyes on him, he proceeds to stoop, serve, suffer and die for the world.

Picture God. The Bible says we should picture a bleeding sacrifice with his arms outstretched, even to his enemies. Is this a God you could believe in?

POURED OUT

I wonder if you're feeling the tension right now? It would be surprising if you weren't. A 'bleeding God' is a mind-boggling concept. Isn't God meant to be above all that? Consider this verse from the Old Testament prophet Isaiah:

For this is what the high and exalted One says—
  he who lives for ever, whose name is holy:
'I live in a high and holy place…' **ISAIAH 57:15**

God is described as exalted, eternal and holy (which means 'sacred' or 'dedicated'). Perhaps this makes us think of God as aloof or remote. But no. The living God is holy—dedicated—but he's dedicated to being a particular kind of God.

Just consider how the verse continues:

'I live in a high and holy place,
  but also with the one who is contrite and lowly in spirit,
to revive the spirit of the lowly
  and to revive the heart of the contrite.' **ISAIAH 57:15**

This is what God—the God Jesus reveals—is like: he moves towards those in need. He doesn't keep himself to himself. He draws near to the hurting, the weary, the struggling. But such movement does not reveal his weakness, it reveals his fullness. God is holy—he is fiercely, blazingly dedicated— to sharing his goodness and life to those without it.

How does this perspective help us as we try to understand a 'bleeding God'? Well, think of a fountain, flowing with life-giving water. You see a fountain's greatness when you see it poured out. And, by parallel, you see God's greatness when you see him poured out *with every drop of his blood*.

When we look at Jesus bleeding to death, we're not seeing something that obscures our view of God. The cross is the clearest possible picture of God, because here is the Source of life giving himself for the world. Jesus' crucifixion is the most divine thing you've ever seen: it's the Fountain poured out.

THE CHAPLAIN'S ANSWER

Perhaps now we can begin to grasp why Private Philips asked his question. With minutes left on earth he wanted to know, 'Is God really like Jesus Christ?' The 19-year-old believed in God but now, about to meet his Maker, he needed to know what this God was like. The 'really' of his question was something he really *needed* to know. Here's how Torrance answered…

> 'The only God that there is, [is] the God who [has] come to
> us in Jesus, shown his face to us, and poured out his love to
> us as our Saviour.'[5]
>
> As Torrance prayed and entrusted the soldier to Jesus'
> safe keeping, Private Philips passed away.

This event became a defining moment in Tom Torrance's
life. He went on to become an eminent church leader and
theologian but all his preaching and writing can be seen as
an answer to that soldier's dying question. Above all else
Torrance was captivated by one biblical idea: that Jesus is
'the radiance of God's glory and the exact representation
of his being' (Hebrews 1:3). Jesus is 'the Word of God'—
the revelation of God—therefore what we see in Jesus is
what we get with God.

This is a truly stunning thought especially when you
consider that Jesus, just like Private Philips, bled out as a
young man. The God who Jesus reveals has arms open to
the world. In fact they were nailed open. Here is a God we
can believe in—a God of astonishing, blood-earnest love.

The poet Byron once said: 'If God is not like Jesus Christ,
he ought to be.' The Bible actually agrees. It just urges
us to complete the thought and rejoice: God *is* like Jesus
Christ. Completely and eternally.

---

5   Alister McGrath, *T. F. Torrance: An Intellectual Biography* (T&T Clarke, 2006), p74.

WATCH

'SAVING PRIVATE PHILIPS'

FOR REFLECTION

- *'Which God don't you believe in?'* How might Tom Wright's question be helpful to ask yourself or others?

- *'Is God really like Jesus Christ?'* How does Tom Torrance's answer give hope, challenge and encouragement?

- What kind of 'picture' of God does Jesus give us?

321

CHAPTER 4

FROM HEAVEN WITH LOVE

WHAT GETS YOU UP?

This is not just a question of what gets you up in the morning—the cat? The kids? Caffeine? It's more a question of your highest motivation. What is tops in the world? What's ultimate? The highest goal to aim towards? Mostly we're just getting by. Here's your chance to pause and ask: What's the absolute best thing in life?

PICTURE THIS:

DEEP IN AN ENCHANTED FOREST, A COUPLE DISCOVER A MYSTERIOUS WELL. IT DOESN'T GRANT THEM THEIR WISHES, IT REVEALS THEM

'It's here,' she says, only half believing it. 'The map was right!'

'For once,' he adds under his breath as she walks ahead into the forest clearing.

Just beyond her he sees it—a simple well of grey stones, rising above the ground about three feet. The waters glow blue-green and emit a hum now audible in the still night air.

'Beautiful!' she says.

Creepy, he thinks.

'Oh look, a plaque!'

Drawing near, he sees it too, on the inside of the well, just above the high waterline. She reads the inscription aloud:

A see-through well to see-through days,
Reflects not here and now.
Instead reveals thy longing gaze,
Not what is seen but how.

Neither know what to say. They let out a disbelieving laugh which quickly turns into a gasp when they look down. Both see it: their reflection, but ten years younger.

'Reveals thy longing gaze,' she says, impressed.

He reaches out towards the image. The moment he touches the waters, it changes. Now he sees himself as a child. He splashes the waters again, now it's his father as a boy.

'Don't,' she says, but he's unable to stop. He stirs the pool as if rubbing out each reflection, but it only gets replaced by an earlier one. Soon there are scenes from the 19th century, the 16th, the 12th. Back and back it goes as he moves the waters—or are the waters moving him?

She joins in, surprised by how heavy and warm the waters feel. The hum grows deeper and louder as the waters churn. The images lose colour as they reverse in time. Soon there are no more people, then no more animals, then no more trees—just a barren earth—then not even that. Finally, like a reverse lightning strike, a brilliant white blaze shoots upwards, blinding them momentarily and knocking them both back onto the grass.

Flat on their backs, they rub their eyes, slowly opening them towards the night sky. The grass is now wet. It wasn't only light that shot up from the well.

'What was that?' she asks breathlessly.

'Life in reverse. Like hitting rewind… *on everything.*'

They hear the hum, now back to its regular tone. The blue-green light is still shimmering, reflected on the leaves of the trees. Clearly the well has more to reveal. One last image, something even more ancient, more fundamental. Not life as it is. Not even life in the beginning—life *before* the beginning.

As they get to their feet, he notices the water level has gone right down. Underneath the original plaque, another is revealed. He reads it:

> *This wishing well, thy wishes tell*
> *That frame what thou wilt see.*
> *Behold the first—thy primal thirst,*
> *This shall be God for thee.*

'What does *that* mean? *What* shall be God for us?' he asks. But she can't hear him. She's walking down the slope from the well along what looks to him to be a dry river bed.

'What are you doing?' he calls.

'Seeing where it leads!' she replies as if it was obvious.

'Where *what* leads?'

'The river of course. The well must have overflowed.'

'Overflowed?' he yells. 'What are you talking about?' He looks down, unable to see any water, unable to see the bottom. 'It's empty,' he cries.

He hears no reply, except those two words echoing back.

IN THE BEGINNING—WHAT?

What do you think was there 'In the beginning'—before people, planets and protons? What would the water in the well show you?

NOTHING

Many would say, *The universe is everything!* And if that's true then before the universe there's nothing, obviously! But it's worth considering how utterly non-obvious this idea is.

Picture nothingness for endless ages. Then nothing turns itself into everything—for no reason. When you think about it, it's the most extraordinary happening ever proposed. As a Christian, I believe in the virgin birth of Jesus, but this would be the virgin birth of the cosmos, and without a virgin—without anything! It's the ultimate magic trick: nothing up the sleeve, no sleeve, no magician, no explanation, just pure magic, out of nowhere.

Even if such a miracle is granted, what would follow from this? How should we consider life's meaning if we've all emerged from nothing?

Perhaps we too should try to fashion something out of nothing. But it's hard to escape the conclusion that, at bottom, it's all meaningless.

CHAOS

Perhaps underneath it all, it's ultimately random. There are forces at play swirling around with no rhyme or reason to anything. We are an accident and we're at the mercy of accidental forces. If this were true what is life's meaning? Fundamentally, it's struggle.

POWER

Alternatively you might say reality is ruled by iron laws of nature that grind along. We're cogs in the machine. Basically our psychology boils down to biology which boils down to chemistry which boils down to physics— molecules clacking together like billiard balls. If this is true then we are, essentially, slaves to impersonal powers.

Religious people can believe in the power thing too. The religious are very prone to imagining God as The Almighty Loner above with nothing and no one beside him—just his own thoughts for company. This 'God' knows nothing of relationship, of back-and-forth, of give-and-take. Such a God simply *is* power. And life is ultimately slavery.

But this is not Jesus' view of things. According to Jesus, in the beginning, there was...

LOVE

When we talk about 'the beginning' it's speculation. When Jesus talked about 'the beginning', it was eye-witness testimony. Jesus said he was there.

The night before he died, Jesus prayed:

> *'Father... you loved me before the creation of the world.'* **JOHN 17:24**

Jesus reckons he is older than the universe—as old as the Father he's praying to. And the picture he paints is of an eternal fountain of love crashing down from the Father to the Son (i.e. to *Jesus)*. Looking into the well we see not nothing, not chaos, not power but an overflowing Source. We see love. And in the very same breath, Jesus prays that his followers would come in on this reality. Here's the verse in full:

> *'Father, I want those you have given me* to be with me
> where I am, *and to see my glory, the glory you have given
> me because you loved me before the creation of the world.'*
>
> **JOHN 17:24, ITALICS MINE**

Jesus wants us to 'be with him where he is'—he wants us
to join him in his life of love.

These words are incredibly lofty—nose-bleed lofty! But
they can ground our deepest intuitions. We all *feel* that love
is the greatest thing. But with Jesus, we can know *why*.

Everyone has a God, of sorts. We all think something is
tops. The question is, What *kind* of God do we have? With
Jesus we see a God of eternal love—a God we can trust.

'THE HEAVENS OPENED'

If 'the heavens open', what do you see? Usually, rain. We
talk about managing to play 17 holes of golf and 'we were
nearly home and dry but *then the heavens opened* and we got
soaked through!' As well as using the phrase in this way,
the Bible uses it more literally to describe *seeing into heaven*.

That's how the phrase is used when describing the baptism
of Jesus. It's a story so crucial it's found in all four of the
Bible's biographies of Jesus.

Let's allow Matthew's Gospel to pull back the curtain
for us. Just five short verses can utterly revolutionise
your vision of God:

Then Jesus came from Galilee to the Jordan [River] to be baptised by John. **MATTHEW 3:13**

Baptism is a ritual wash. You get washed on the outside because you're saying, 'I need a power shower of the heart, a cleansing that is soul-deep.' We might believe in a God of love, but that doesn't mean everything is lovely. It's not. And *we're* not. We're not the loving people we should be. Those queuing up for baptism were recognising that this 'unloveliness' is not just *out there* in the world. It's in them too. So they stand in line to take a bath. And John is there to help.

The John mentioned here is John the Baptist. He's a different John to the one who wrote John's Gospel. It was a common name back then (just as it is today). So John the Baptist is doing the dunking and it's incredibly popular. People are queuing up to take a bath. This is basically a 'Failures Convention'. Everyone's very welcome, the one qualification for this bath is the admission that you need one. And as they all line up, admitting their failures, who should show up except the perfect, pure Son of God? This is a shock. Jesus is the one person who doesn't need a bath. So...

...John tried to deter him, saying, 'I need to be baptised by you, and do you come to me?' **MATTHEW 3:14**

Why would Jesus take a bath? He's been in on the Fountain of love from the beginning. Why is he joining the 'Failures Convention'?

> *Jesus replied, 'Let it be so now; it is proper for us to do this to fulfil all righteousness.' Then John consented.* **MATTHEW 3:15**

Jesus is saying, 'It might seem wrong, but it's actually right—right in the deepest sense. This is the way it has to be. I join you in your failures, so you can join me in my family.' And as Jesus goes through the waters, we get the most beautiful picture of this family:

> *As soon as Jesus was baptised, he went up out of the water. At that moment heaven was opened, and Jesus saw the Spirit of God descending like a dove and alighting on him. And a voice from heaven said, 'This is my Son, whom I love; with him I am well pleased.'* **MATTHEW 3:16–17**

If the heavens opened, what would you see? This! Here is the Niagara Falls of love: The Father full of praise for his Son and filling him with the Holy Spirit. If you wound back the clock to life 'in the beginning' this is what you would find:

> *God is a loving union of THREE: The Father, the Son and the Holy Spirit.*

There is only one God. And this one God is a loving union of THREE: the Father, Son and Holy Spirit. To encounter any of these THREE is to encounter God—not 'one third of God', but God at full strength!

Yet, if you encounter any of the THREE, the other two are intimately involved. That's because the THREE are never apart. So to encounter Jesus is to encounter his Father and his Spirit. They are not *individuals* with their own life to lead who work together on occasion. Instead, there is one life of God—one unbreakable unity. And it's a *loving* unity. Those words from heaven describe the very heartbeat of God's life: 'This is my Son, whom I love, with him I am well pleased.'

Here at Jesus' baptism we clearly see that Jesus is not the Father—Jesus is being baptised in the Jordan River while the Father speaks from heaven. Throughout the Gospels we see Jesus talking to his Father and being filled with the Spirit. The THREE are one, but they are not the same *person*. Instead the THREE are bound forever in one mission, one purpose, one life, one love – one essence. For this reason the Bible does not just say that God is loving. God *is* loving. But it says something far deeper: 'God *is* love' (1 John 4:8). Eternally the Father has loved his Son in the joy of the Spirit.

Perhaps you've heard the word 'Trinity' before. That's what we're talking about here. Don't let the word put you off, it's just a way of squashing two words together:

God is an unbreakable and eternal unity of THREE. In other words he's a THREE-UNITY… a TRI-UNITY… a TRINITY. We shouldn't be put off by the word, we should be wowed by the reality: There is a perfect unity before and behind the universe: one God, supreme in all things. And this one God *is* love.

The truth about 'Trinity' is not a maths problem to be solved. It's the good news that God is love, and you're invited.

WATCH

'FROM HEAVEN WITH LOVE'

FOR REFLECTION

- 'Nothing, Chaos, Power or Love', how do *you* picture 'the beginning'?

- How does the idea of THREE relate to the idea that 'God is love'?

- What do you find difficult about the idea of God being a loving union of THREE? What do you find attractive?

OPTIONAL READING PART 2

JOHN CHAPTERS 8—14

QUESTIONS FOR REFLECTION:

- How are people responding to Jesus? Why?

- What kind of things is Jesus saying and doing to reveal his own identity?

- What does Jesus teach about his death and resurrection?

- How does Jesus reveal the Father and the Spirit in these chapters?

THE WORLD'S TWO-NESS

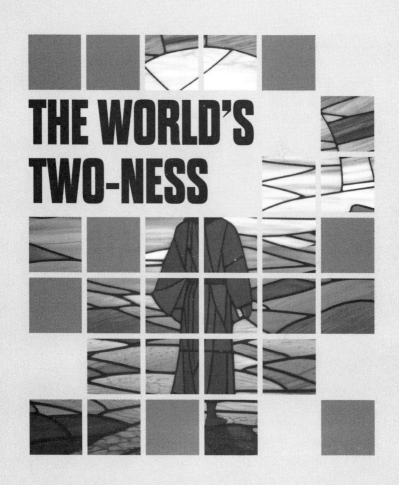

CHAPTER 5

FALLING DOWN

WHAT GETS YOU DOWN?

It could be big or small, a pet peeve or a profound grief, a problem out in the world, or a problem in our own life: What are your nightmare scenarios? What are your big regrets and complaints? What disappoints you, defeats you or depresses you?

PICTURE THIS:

LATE AT NIGHT A CLEANER SWEEPS THE STAGE OF AN EMPTY THEATRE WHEN SUDDENLY...

It began out of nerves; it continued out of boredom. Each night, while he swept the stage, the cleaner would sing the show's opening number:

Look down, look down, der der der dum dum dee,
Look down, look down, sher, sher, sher, dun dee dee...

He never did learn the lines. Still, not a bad baritone, he thought. Not quite solo material but if the chorus was ever short of a singer, he'd make sure he was on hand.

Just as he began to imagine the scenario he heard a click from way up 'in the gods'. All at once his eyes were flooded with light and his blood with adrenaline. His nerves crunched as did his body, retreating from the spotlight instinctively.

Who else is in the theatre? How long have they been here? What have they seen? What have I been doing? Is this about my singing? My work? My immigration status? My...

Each anxiety felt like a rip tide, carrying him further out to sea.

He didn't dare move as his eyes darted around the theatre. He saw nothing, which made the command even more alarming.

'Step into the light.'

The voice was unfamiliar and he couldn't tell its direction. It was neither friendly nor threatening. It simply expected compliance.

He waited. Perhaps further instruction would come. Or explanation. Nothing. And the silence seemed to add more weight than words ever could. What to do?

To obey felt both simple and momentous, both expected and impossible. The light did not seem safe. But neither did the darkness.

He was afraid the spot would shift and pick out his hunched form. He was equally afraid that the light would depart and leave him to the gloom. So, clutching his broom like a shield, he hovered between the two.

What would you do?

There's something attractive and compelling about 'stepping into the light'. We're drawn to light in many ways. But then, there's something terrifying too. The light exposes us—reveals things we've kept concealed. Even the biggest show-offs soon discover how unflattering the limelight can be.

We're conflicted. There's a part of us that loves the light and a part that fears it—hates it, even. There's a part of us that wants to be seen, and a part of us that really doesn't. We're split in two. And that split-ness—that TWO-ness—defines our world and defines our lives.

WHERE ARE WE UP TO?

So far in *How to See Life: A Guide in 321*, we've met Jesus and started to see how he illuminates all things for us. We've seen *his* picture of God. God is a loving union of THREE: the Father, the Son and the Holy Spirit.

This means that God is love. He is a Fountain of light, life and love. There has *always* been a Father loving his Son in the joy of the Holy Spirit. It means we've come from love, we've been shaped by love, we're intended for love. That's good news.

But in this section we turn our attention to the world. And that's a very mixed picture. Sometimes we see things as they ought to be—glimpses of light, life and love. But look again and you will see the world as it *is*. So much of the world is spoiled, marred, twisted.

- It ought to be full of light, but all around there is darkness.

- It ought to be full of life, but we're surrounded by death.

- It ought to be full of love, but it's shot through with disconnection—that is, the failure to connect, the failure to relate, the failure to love.

The world is not as it should be. And, let's get personal, we are not who we should be either. There's a split between the way things *ought to be* and the way they *actually are*—between the way *I* ought to be and the way *I* naturally am.

In the Bible, these two realities are represented by two people. The way life ought to be is represented by Jesus. The way things are is represented by Adam—the first man in the Bible. Our whole world is shaped by these two representatives.

ADAM: LIFE AS IT IS

Adam pops up right at the beginning of the Bible's first book, Genesis, and he gives us a profound picture of life as it is. Adam's story shows us what's wrong with the world and what's wrong with ourselves.

In Hebrew, the language of the Old Testament, the word 'Adam' simply means humanity. His story is our story. It's the sense of: 'There was once a guy called Humanity. And Humanity had a lot going for him but then Humanity screwed everything up and it all fell apart.' Adam is a representative—our representative. What he does in the story, we're always doing in our lives.

So what did he do?

We begin in a garden paradise; it's all golden. 'The man and his wife [Eve] were both naked and they felt no shame' (Genesis 2:25). While Genesis chapter 1 presents the creation of the world, Genesis chapter 2 zooms in on the creation of Humanity. It presents a royal couple, Adam and Eve, king and queen of all the world—in paradise and in love. Essentially God places Humanity in his world and says: 'You run it.' He gives Humanity every fruit from every tree, it's all delicious, it's all beautiful, it's all free. At this stage there's just one tree off limits.

Adam and Eve live the most rule-free existence anyone has ever known, but there is *one* boundary—one forbidden fruit. They can go anywhere and do anything, but there is one way Humanity can tell God 'Count me out of life with you.' You might wonder why God would do this, but consider the alternative. If there is literally no way of telling God, 'I'm out', then there's no genuine way of telling him 'I'm in' either.

So God gives them one opportunity. If they want *in*, all they have to do is refrain from one thing in all the world. Simply steer clear of that one forbidden fruit and all will be well.

You *know* how the story goes, don't you? You don't need any biblical knowledge. You don't need to have heard of Adam and Eve. You can predict what happens next because you know how stories go and you know what Humanity is like. Sure enough, Genesis chapter 2 gives way to Genesis chapter 3, and we read of what we now call 'the fall'.

As we watch Humanity descend through these familiar steps, I'm sure they'll resonate with you. We begin where all relational breakdown begins…

SUSPICION

Temptation comes, in the form of a serpent.

> *Now the snake was more crafty than any of the wild animals the LORD God had made.* **GENESIS 3:1**

At this point we all ask, who is this serpent? Later on in the Bible he becomes known as Satan or the devil or the tempter. Here, it's early days. He's presented as one more creature in the world—highly intelligent, deeply curious. He's feeling out Humanity and Humanity is answering. A dance begins, back and forth. But the first step is suspicion. Listen as the snake sows doubt in the minds of Humanity:

> *'Did God really say, "You must not eat from any tree in the garden"?'* **GENESIS 3:1**

Actually Humanity could eat from any tree except this one. God's emphasis is on the bounty. The serpent fixes on the boundary. He continues:

> *'God knows that when you eat from it your eyes will be opened, and you will be like God, knowing good and evil.'* **GENESIS 3:5**

Here's the temptation: Be suspicious—consider that God is holding out on you. Forget the fullness you're enjoying, fixate on what's forbidden.

Adam and Eve listened and their trust in God's goodness evaporated. But Adam represents us all. We don't usually think of God as a Fountain of life. More usually we consider him a miser, dishing out necessities with a teaspoon and a scowl. I don't know about you, but I relate to Adam.

And then suspicion ripens to selfishness as suddenly God doesn't look so good anymore.

SELFISHNESS

> *When the woman saw that the fruit of the tree was good for food and pleasing to the eye, and also desirable for gaining wisdom, she took some and ate it. She also gave some to her husband, who was with her, and he ate it.* **GENESIS 3:6**

Adam and Eve don't trust their Maker, so they grasp selfishly at life for themselves, no matter the consequences. That's the story of Humanity: suspicion leading to selfishness.

As we grasp at the stuff of life, we try to get our joy, security and significance from those things. The snake promised an experience of 'eye-opening' wonder. And that's the fulfilment we're always chasing. We think to ourselves, 'If I can only get *that*…' If I get that job, that relationship, that holiday, that achievement, that money, that experience… I'll be satisfied.

But that quest becomes all-consuming.

SLAVERY

> *Then the eyes of both of them were opened, and they realised they were naked; so they sewed fig leaves together and made coverings for themselves.* **GENESIS 3:7**

When Adam and Eve get the thing they'd grasped at, they hoped for an eye-opening moment of true fulfilment. But all they see is how much they lack, how unsatisfied they are, how naked they are.

This is life isn't it? We live for people's love. We live for people's respect. We live for the weekend. But those things don't ultimately satisfy. We're like thirsty explorers looking for satisfaction, going from one broken fountain to the next, thinking '*This time!*'

It doesn't work, and as we go from achievement to relationships to status to sex to money to power to distraction to drugs to experiences to this person to that person, nothing works. We aim at the perfect career, the perfect family, the perfect body: it's a *slavery*. And the one thing that could break the spell of these substitute gods is the one thing Humanity refuses to do. They refuse to come clean and admit their mistakes.

SELF-JUSTIFICATION

Then the man and his wife heard the sound of the LORD God as he was walking in the garden in the cool of the day, and they hid from the LORD God among the trees of the garden. But the LORD God called to the man, 'Where are you?'

He answered, 'I heard you in the garden, and I was afraid because I was naked; so I hid.'

And he said, 'Who told you that you were naked? Have you eaten from the tree from which I commanded you not to eat?'

The man said, 'The woman you put here with me—she gave me some fruit from the tree, and I ate it.'

Then the LORD God said to the woman, 'What is this you have done?'

The woman said, 'The snake deceived me, and I ate.' **GENESIS 3:8-13**

Here is a comedy masterclass in blame-shifting. *'She did it.'* *'God, it's your fault.'* *'The devil made me do it.'*

The comedian George Carlin used to joke that when you're driving everyone slower than you is an *idiot*, everyone faster than you is a *maniac*—but you drive just right, don't you? Self-justification! It's so stupid and so human. And it leaves us with a tragically funny vision of Humanity— guilty blaggers, covering their tracks and trying to talk their way out of trouble. Self-justifying fools who hastily paint over their wrong-ness with a thin veneer of right- ness. But in the end, Humanity is left with its own self- inflicted demise.

SCREW-UPS

In this story, Humanity knows where the self-destruct button is. It's really well labelled, the warnings are clear. But the way the story's told you get the sense of Humanity racing over to the self-destruct button and slamming it for all its worth. And you think, *how ridiculous!* Yes it is. But also, *how relatable!*

I'll speak for myself, but I suspect you'll know what I'm talking about. I sabotage my own happiness, continually. I sabotage my own success too. I manage to sabotage it better than anyone else. I am my own worst enemy. And then, out of the blue, I'll turn on you if you get too close. I'll say things or do things in my worst moments that are appalling and I'll want to self-justify. I'll say 'I'm sorry I did that, I'm sorry I said that, I don't know what came over me.' But of course nothing came over me. All that stuff came out of me. It came out of somewhere very deep, very dark and very old.

Can you relate?

Then maybe we're related! Maybe we're part of this family of Adam and maybe we all share in these family traits. That's what the Bible says. We're all part of a dysfunctional family—the human family. And no one can pretend to have a different human nature. No one has a pure, pristine humanity.

In a deep sense we're all in the same boat: Adam's boat. What he did in the story, we do in our lives. Constantly. We all share his suspicion, selfishness, slavery, self-justification and screw-ups. This is what the Bible means by sin.

SIN

When people hear the word 'sin', sometimes they think of outrageous crimes that might land you in prison. Others think of trivial naughtiness—a crude joke, a white lie, cheating on your diet. In the Bible, sin is a condition—a congenital disorder that never skips a generation. We're born into this dysfunctional family and we *all* share the family likeness. Some people are better than others at concealing and containing their sin but everyone carries the disorder. And it's fatal.

'To dust you will return,' says God to Humanity in Genesis chapter 3. 'For the wages of sin is death,' says the New Testament writer Paul (Romans 6:23). And it makes sense: if God is life, to reject him is death. It's the nature of the case. And it's the nature of humanity. We are sinners and that means we're all caught up in the darkness, death and disconnection of this world.

You may have questions about whether the Adam story is true. You may have questions about whether it's fair. In the FAQs we will address that. But let me first ask you to consider: is the Adam story *happening*? Does it ring true to your experience of the world and your experience of yourself?

We began with the idea of a spotlight shining from above. Having heard Adam's story, let me ask you: *Do you want to step into the light? Are you prepared to be seen—and to be seen as a sinner?*

It's never comfortable. We don't like to be seen. Adam and Eve hid. They made fig leaf coverings. But nothing changes until we stop hiding and step into the light. So let me encourage you to be honest. The way forward is to forget the fig leaves and come clean. Our hope is not in managing or minimising our sin. As we'll see in the next chapter, our hope comes from beyond—from a Saviour: the *Second* Adam.

'FALLING DOWN'

FOR REFLECTION

- Do you recognise yourself in the Adam story? How so?

- How do you see suspicion, selfishness, slavery, self-justification and screw-ups relating to each other? How do you see them relating to you?

- How do you feel about the idea that everyone shares these family traits, everyone is a sinner?

CHAPTER 6

UP!

WHAT IS WRONG WITH THE WORLD?

We can probably all agree that something is wrong with the world, but what? Is the problem with individuals, society, economics, politics, the environment? Is it about forces 'out there' in the world, or 'in here' in human nature? How do you finish the sentence, 'The world is in a mess because…'?

PICTURE THIS:

A MAN FALLS INTO A DEEP HOLE. TRY AS HE MIGHT, HE CAN'T CLIMB OUT

'Help' comes the cry and eventually it meets the ears of a passer-by.

The mystic peers down and says, 'Hush child, there is no hole. The hole is an illusion,' and then leaves.

Time passes and a religious leader comes along: 'You should have listened to me,' he scolds, then leaves.

A social media influencer flits past: 'Thoughts and prayers,' and then leaves.

A politician looks down and says: 'This hole was the other party's fault.'

A pragmatist says, 'Just climb up.' A cynic says 'You're probably better off down there.' An idealist says, 'Look on the bright side.'

But they all leave. And our guy is left with a bunch of good advice and no way out.

Finally a friend comes. He does what friends do. He hears, he draws near, he dives in. He gets hurt, he gets dirty. But he hoists the man onto his shoulders and lifts him out.

Jesus is that Friend. We are in a pit but Jesus joins us.

There are many religions in the world, many life philosophies. And there is much good advice in them. But Jesus is different. In Christianity there is not just advice from on high. In Christianity, the God who is above comes down below, and not simply for a brief visit. He comes down to live our life for us, die our death for us and rise again for us. The story of Jesus shows us what *God* is like. It also shows us what *we* are like.

A HELL OF A PIT

When you think about it, walking away from God is doubly wrong: it's both ridiculous and rebellious. In the Old Testament, God addresses his people like this:

'My people have committed two sins: They have forsaken me, the spring of living water, and have dug their own cisterns [wells], broken cisterns that cannot hold water.' **JEREMIAH 2:13**

It's an analogy. The people weren't literally digging wells, but God is constantly getting us to 'picture this'. And it's worth pressing in—imagine the people in a desert wasteland, scouring the horizon for an oasis. Behind them bubbles an inexhaustible Fountain, bursting with life. But they press on towards the horizon, shovels in hand. Some dig in one place, some in another, all dying of thirst. In their efforts, the best they manage is a mouthful of mud, and all the while the Fountain gushes in easy reach.

The people are committing 'two sins'. They are ridiculous well-diggers *and* they are rebellious God-forsakers. And this is our nature too. It is really foolish to reject God. It's also really nasty. Of course it's a stupid strategy but it's also a hurtful rejection. We have 'forsaken' a God who is the Source of our life—a God who longs for us like a parent for a lost child.

For many of us, our worst moments as children came when we told our mum or dad, 'I hate you, I hate this family, I wish I was never born.' The Bible says, we've all done that cosmically. And that's not just childish. It's personal. It's an offence to the God who made us. We are all the kind of people who walk away from light, life and love. We are all the kind of people who walk away from God.

So here we lie fallen in this pit. We have rebelled against the very Source of our lives. And if you forsake light, life and love, you *will* find yourself in darkness, death and disconnection. That's where humanity *is* but it's vital we don't *remain* here.

Jesus speaks of our disconnection as stretching on beyond our earthly life, because all of us go on beyond our earthly life. And Jesus describes that fate in terms of outer darkness, of being lost, of being shut out from the feast of heaven, with tears of sorrow and bitterness.

I don't know if you believe in hell, but Jesus did.

He believed in it enough to do something extraordinary. He came down.

JESUS: LIFE AS IT'S MEANT TO BE

The central idea for this section is the truth of TWO:

The world is shaped by TWO representatives: Adam and Jesus.

Last chapter we saw how Adam represents humanity. His suspicion, selfishness, slavery, self-justification and screw-ups encapsulate the world as it is. It's not pretty. And it has no future. Adam falls—and he falls into a hole he can't climb out of. Thank God there is a *second* representative!

Jesus is the answer to Adam—he's the good-Adam, the second Adam. If Adam represents life as it is in its disconnection, Jesus represents life as it's meant to be: a life of love. And so, of course, he does what love does. When he sees us in the pit, of course he befriends us. Of course he draws near and pays whatever it costs to save us.

Where the first Adam takes us down to the pit, the Second Adam, Jesus, dives into the pit to lift us up.

Essentially the Gospels are the record of what happened when love came down. Here comes an Almighty Friend. A true Saviour. And here comes a true picture of Humanity—God's answer to Adam:

As you read the Gospels you can ask yourself...

- Was Jesus suspicious? No, he's the Son of God, he has always trusted his Father.

- Was Jesus selfish? No, he's the servant of all. He is love covered over with flesh.

- Was Jesus enslaved? No, he is the free-est man who ever lived. He didn't have an ounce of earthly power yet he walked around with unparalleled courage, presence and fearlessness.

- Was Jesus self-justifying? No, even when they arrested him on trumped up charges and tried him as a criminal, he didn't defend himself. As they crucified him he prayed 'Father, forgive.'

- Did Jesus screw up? Not once. Which is remarkable! Every other member of Adam's family screws up every day. Jesus lived the life that we should live without a single blemish.

And then, on the cross, he died the death that we should die. The Bible says:

> [Christ] *suffered once for sins, the righteous for the unrighteous, to bring you to God.* **1 PETER 3:18**

He did what love does. Love takes a bullet for the one they love. Love says, 'Your darkness will be my darkness, your debts will be my debts, your sins will be my sins, your hell will be my hell.' This is why Christians love Jesus.

The First Adam went to his tree in the Garden of Eden and brought death for the world. Christ went to his tree—the cross—to bring life to the world. Adam's path was down into the pit. Christ's path takes him *through* the pit and up into life. That's the meaning of the Easter weekend: On Good Friday, Jesus dies our death as our representative. He takes our hell. But on Easter Sunday, Jesus rises again *as our representative*, to give us his heaven.

The Bible puts it like this:

> *Since death came through a man, the resurrection of the dead comes also through a man. For as in Adam all die, so in Christ all will be made alive.*
> **1 CORINTHIANS 15:21–22**

We're all born into Adam's kind of life. But here is the offer: *be born again* into Christ's kind of life.

Perhaps you've heard that phrase: 'born again'. This is what it means: we were born once into Adam's family—family number one. And it's a dysfunctional family! But Christ has joined our family, so we can join *his*. If we come to Jesus we are born again into family number two. Having shared in Adam's kind of life, we now also share in Jesus' kind of life. We get his Father as our Father, his Spirit as our Spirit and his brothers and sisters in the church as our brothers and sisters.

In this way, the world is shaped by TWO representatives: Adam and Jesus. We were born once into the family of Adam, we are born again into the family of Jesus.

FACING UP

Perhaps this section of the book has been a shock. It's never comfortable to hear that you're in trouble. Think of our opening story in this chapter: the man who fell down a hole. Even as you picture the scene, you're probably not all the way down in the pit looking up. If you're anything like me, you're probably imagining yourself up on the surface (even if you have sympathy for the poor unfortunate *down there*). We rarely think ourselves into a hopeless plight. We identify more with the advisors on high, competent and wise. And even if we admit we're in a fix right now, we tend to believe we can solve it. If only we can summon up the strength or the resources, we reckon we can figure it out.

Most of us try to do what psychologist Larry Crabb called our default strategy for life: *we try to look good in the presence of judgement*. We manage. We cope. With all eyes on us, we cover our worst sins and put our best foot forward. We don't want to look inadequate or foolish or wrong.

But trying to look good in the presence of judgement is a life of pressure and performance. It's not the good life Jesus came to give us. According to the Bible we do not climb out of the pit. We can't. Jesus comes down. He is the 'Friend of sinners'. That's a title that Jesus gladly owns in the Bible (Luke 7:34). It means that our sins don't keep him away. Our sins draw him near.

In the presence of this Friend we can name our Adam-like sins: our selfishness and screw-ups. Real change happens when we drop the act and get real. Our Friend—the Lord Jesus—has descended to our depths. Now, instead of *looking good in the presence of judgement*, we can *look bad in the presence of love*. That's where true healing is.

WATCH

'UP!'

FOR REFLECTION

- How are Jesus and Adam similar? How are they different?

- If Jesus is the Friend who joins us in the pit, how does this give us hope for the world?

- We've covered some difficult issues, discussing 'sin' and 'hell'. How does this teaching about Adam and Jesus cast light on these topics?

OPTIONAL READING PART 3

JOHN CHAPTERS 15—21

QUESTIONS FOR REFLECTION:

- What does Jesus say about the THREE (i.e. himself, his Father and the Holy Spirit)? How do the THREE relate to each other? How do the THREE relate to the believer?

- How do these chapters reveal the split-ness or TWO-ness of the world? What does Jesus do to help us with that TWO-ness?

- How do these chapters reveal the believer's ONE-ness—with Jesus, and with each other?

- Chapter 20 verse 31 says that John's Gospel was 'written so that you might believe'. Do you believe? What has been your response to Jesus?

YOUR ONE-NESS

CHAPTER 7

CHAMPION

WHAT GETS YOU THROUGH?

When you've finished describing what gets you down, what comes next? Perhaps you say, 'Still... worse things happen at sea.' Or 'Still... I'm better off than some, got to count my blessings.' Or 'Still... I've only got myself to blame.' Or 'Still... at least I have my health, or my family, or my...' What are your consolations in life? Your helps? Your sustaining graces?

PICTURE THIS:

A FOOTBALL CLUB IS HEADED FOR DISASTER BUT ONE FAN CAN SEE A WAY FORWARD.[6]

The hotel conference room is a tangle of cables, camera tripods and lighting rigs. Harrison is helped by his dad to their reserved seats in the front row. There's even a spot for his walker. The club may be last in the Premier League but their commitment to disability inclusion remained first rate. Harrison was even promised the chance to ask a question—the seventh and final question of the press conference. He'd been mulling it over all week.

---

6 Based very loosely on the story of Jack Grealish and Finlay Fisher.

He didn't want to ask something obvious. He was only 11 but he knew what angle the journalists would take. They'd ask whether the new signing was too old. They'd ask if he felt the pressure of the price tag. They'd ask about his fitness given all his many injuries. They'd ask about adjusting to English conditions when he's only played in South America. They'd ask about whether the club could avoid relegation. They'd ask whether he was an expensive gamble in a lost cause. Harrison, though, had a different question and while he was practising it under his breath, the announcer sitting behind the bank of microphones cleared his throat.

'Ladies and gentlemen, we are very pleased to announce our latest signing. He's a phenomenal talent and a born leader. We are thrilled to introduce him to you for the first time wearing the red and gold, please will you welcome our new number 9: Felipe Sosa!'

Only Harrison claps as his hero appears, shorter than he imagined. The rest of the room fills with the photographers' shouts: 'Felipe!' 'Over here!' A thousand shots are taken before Felipe settles into his chair and the reporters settle into their interrogation.

The questions are even more sceptical than Harrison predicted. Sosa answers with smiles and some rehearsed lines about his newfound love of the club. Harrison is mesmerised by the accent. Every time the

Argentine says 'very, very', he copies under his breath while his father chuckles. After six questions, the floor is Harrison's. All falls silent as a woman runs a handheld mic to his seat.

'Felipe,' he squeaks, and then stops. He starts again lowering his voice. 'Felipe, I'm Harrison and I have cerebral palsy. I heard your daughter has cerebral palsy. Is that true? And are you a good dad to her?'

The question seems to surprise everyone except Felipe. He smiles. 'I hope so. You have to ask her.' He adds, 'Are you a good son to your dad?'

'Occasionally!' his dad calls out to ripples of laughter.

'Ah I see,' says Felipe turning to Harrison and narrowing his eyes, 'and is he a good dad?'

'Sometimes!' says Harrison, getting his own back. 'But he never lets me win. We play football in the back garden but I can't beat him.'

'Ah! You need a… team mate,' says Felipe searching for the words. 'Why don't I join your team, I think we can win then, yes?'

Harrison beams at the thought. 'Yeah! Then we can do the robot.'

Some are chuckling. Felipe frowns: 'Do the robot, what is this?'

'My goal celebration,' explains Harrison showing the room his best moves.

'Ah, I see! Very, very good,' says Felipe. 'I will tell you something. Harrison, is it?'

'M-hm,' he says, mid-robot.

'OK, Harrison. You heard the questions they ask today. No one here thinks our team will stay up. But you do, don't you?'

'Yeah!' says Harrison, as though it's the most obvious thing in the world.

'So that's two of us. And, now, well, this may sound crazy but we are still in the FA cup, yes?'

Harrison nods, marvelling at the fact Felipe Sosa just said 'we' about *his team*.

'Well I say we are going to stay up *and*,' he goes on jabbing the air with his finger, 'I say we are going to win the cup.' Scoffing erupts in the room but Felipe continues, 'And when we do—*when we do*—I will do the robot for you, OK? How's that?'

Harrison simply nods, wide-eyed, while the announcer wraps up the press conference: 'That's all we have time for ladies and gentlemen...' Sosa leaves with the manager. Harrison buries his head in his father's chest. 'I can't believe it!' he says. 'I can't believe it!'

Ironically, he's the only one in the room who does.

JOINING THE TEAM

Three chapters ago we considered the baptism of Jesus. Until then he'd been a carpenter in a northern backwater of Israel. But at the Jordan River, he became a public figure, introduced to the world. Everyone was there to confess their sins and have a ceremonial wash—a baptism. But Jesus chooses this Failures Convention to be his launch event.

Just like Felipe Sosa's press conference, the baptism of Jesus was the moment he shook hands with 'the manager', so to speak. The Father declares to the world: 'This is my Son—this is The One!' Jesus is publicly identified with God his Father. *And* he's publicly identified with us, his sinful people.

Think of Felipe Sosa putting on the team shirt: he's shouldering their burdens. He's saying to the club, *I identify with you in your struggle. From now on, I represent you, even with all your problems.* As Sosa takes responsibility for his team so Jesus shoulders the burdens of Team Adam.

As we have seen in the last section, Team Adam is a failing team, headed for relegation. None of us are good at the game of life. Left to ourselves we routinely fail at the challenges we face and our arch rival, death, always wins. We need someone to turn it all around. We need a Champion.

So Jesus comes to us as an Almighty Felipe Sosa. He enters our plight to bring the most astonishing victory. Just imagine how the story runs.

A week after the press conference, Sosa plays his first game: an away match against their arch rivals. He scores three times, silencing the home crowd. And so begins a season that can only be described as fairytale.

In game after game, Sosa produces a superhuman performance, lifting his team out of the relegation zone and into safety. In the FA Cup, he continually pulls out the winner when all looks lost. He propels his team all the way to Wembley.

And there is Harrison. Of course he's there. Of course he's proudly wearing the number 9 shirt. And of course his father is wearing it too—he, like everyone else, has come around to Sosa's magic.

The cup final is an epic battle, fast and physical. They are reduced to 10 men and then 9 as, controversially, two of Sosa's team mates are sent off. Then late in the second half it looks like they'll lose Sosa too. He pulls his Achilles—again!—but he refuses to come off the pitch. He limps on. He wants, it seems, to see out this brave defeat. They've been behind for 93 minutes of the match. And then… well, you know how fairytale seasons go.

In the final minute of added time Felipe scores twice to snatch victory from the jaws of defeat. The roar is deafening, unlike anything Harrison has ever heard or ever will. Sosa runs the full length of the pitch to his supporters' end. And there—in front of the crowd, in front of the cameras, in front of Harrison—he does the robot. Everyone does.

Imagine you're Harrison: how do you feel?

Ecstatic? Euphoric? Words fail at this point. My emotional range usually runs between 'fine' and 'not too bad'. Occasionally it descends to 'don't ask' or rises all the way to 'good actually'. But the joys we're talking about here burst through the containers in which we keep our hopes.

At certain points in life our feelings can go higher than we'd thought possible—and wider. *Everyone* shares in this joy. When Felipe scores that goal, millions share in the euphoria. Many will celebrate even more than the footballer himself!

We share a mysterious connection with the champion and we share a mysterious connection with each other. We may just hug a complete stranger because they're wearing the same shirt as us—the same shirt as *him*. We're all celebrating the same victory because we all share the same hero. We have not expended a calorie of effort in the victory, but we carry on like we scored the winner. He wins, we celebrate.

And this is how Christians feel about Jesus.

THE MATCH REPORTS

This is perhaps the most helpful way to read the Gospels. They are the match reports of Jesus taking on our arch rivals. Time and again he pulls off a victory while we look on, hearts in our mouths. He takes on temptation… and he resists it. He takes on sickness… and he heals it. He takes on the chaotic forces of nature… and he calms them. He takes on evil powers… and he drives them out.

All these forces are far bigger than us. We lose to them every time. But not Jesus. And then on the cross Jesus shoulders our darkness, our death and our disconnection. On Good Friday, Jesus represents us in all our sin, our guilt and our shame. He takes responsibility for it all and takes it down to the hell that it deserves.

To the onlookers it might have seemed like Jesus had lost. But no. On Easter Sunday, we see the ultimate comeback. He bursts out of the grave as the victor over sin, death and hell. And he comes to us like a footballer to his fans saying, *It's for you, it's for you!* His victory is our victory. He wins, we celebrate—though we have not expended a calorie of effort.

This is the beating heart of the Christian story. Later in the Bible, Paul (who wrote half the New Testament) can hardly contain himself as he reflects on this: 'thanks be to God! He gives us the victory through our Lord Jesus Christ' (1 Corinthians 15:57).

JESUS—COACH OR CHAMPION?

The world is full of coaches. There are any number of people who will tell you how to live. There is wisdom out there for how *you* can get through this world—how *you* can navigate the obstacles in your life. Maybe now you can think of the coaches that help you get by. Without doubt many of them will give you good advice. But Jesus is not, fundamentally, a coach. This is a surprise to many.

Very often people will think of Jesus (or of God or of Christianity) as a guide shouting instruction from heaven or from a holy book. Such advice may help you play the game of life a little better. Ultimately though, win or lose, it's down to you.

If you think you're quite good at the game of life, this might sound OK. Maybe you only want a coach to fine-tune your performance.

But, I'll speak for myself: I am *not* good at the game of life. Of course, I can often fool myself that I'm doing all right, but then something will happen which highlights my selfishness, pride, anger, greed or malice. I have deep regrets and have known gnawing guilt and shame. I am weak, I am dying, and one day I will face my Maker.

It's all too much. I can't handle any of these things by myself. I don't just need a coach, I need a champion. I need a saviour. But a saviour is exactly who we are offered:

- Do you have regrets about your past? Jesus says, *I take your past, I nail it to the cross and I give you my future.*

- Do you have shame? Jesus says: *I endured burning shame and I buried it forever. Now I've risen beyond it to give you new life with your head held high.*

- Do you despair of your sinful nature? Jesus says: *I became sin on that cross and I rise to give you my Spirit.*

- Do you fear death? Jesus says: *I have taken that ultimate death—the deadly judgement of God against sin—I have died it for you. Now let me lead you through the troubles of life and into eternity.*

Jesus does not yell advice from heaven, he takes our side. He joins Team Adam, not because *he* is a failure, he's sinless. He joins in order to take responsibility for all *our* failures. He represents us. In this sense Jesus is our Champion. *He actually secures the win for us.*

Therefore now, if you're on Team Jesus, your life is caught up with his. You share in Jesus' Father, his Spirit, his future, and his victory. He is not so much a coach, far more he's a Champion. And Christianity is not so much good advice: it's good news.

> *Thanks be to God! He gives us the victory through our Lord Jesus Christ.* **1 CORINTHIANS 15:57**

WATCH

'CHAMPION'

FOR REFLECTION

- How would you describe Jesus? Has your view changed over time?

- What do you make of the difference between a coach and a champion, and between good advice and good news?

- How would you describe a Christian? Has your view changed? How do you think those around you view Christians today?

CHAPTER 8

LOVE STORY

WHAT IS A CHRISTIAN?

If someone tells you they are a Christian, what do you assume about them? What does it mean to be a Christian? Is your answer about beliefs, behaviour, habits, culture? How do you finish this sentence: 'A Christian is someone who...'?

PICTURE THIS:

THE LOVE STORY BETWEEN A SECRET KING AND THE PAUPER HE LOVES.[7]

In peasant's shawl the King came low,

To meet the one he loved,

He stooped to stations far below,

Those lofty courts above.

He knew his pomp would sure prevent,

Her freely-given hand.

She could not yield a true assent,

If pressed by royal command.

And so in all humility,

7 Based on the parable of the king and the maiden, from Søren Kierkegaard, *Philosophical Fragments,* antilogicalism.com/wp-content/uploads/2017/07/philosophical-fragments.pdf, p14.

He full-assumed her rank.

To years of vulnerability,

And bended knee he sank.

She gladly wed the secret King

And on that day was seen—

The King who gave up everything

And pauper turned a Queen.

ALL THAT I AM

When my wife and I married, we said these vows from the Church of England marriage service:

'All that I am I give to you, all that I have I share with you.'

At that moment there were sniggers in the congregation. Our friends were laughing because they knew we had absolutely nothing to offer each other. Essentially we were pledging to unite our debts. It was very romantic!

But think about the fairytale wedding. When the Pauper and the King become one there's a wonderful turn of events. He gladly absorbs her debts and she gratefully receives his life.

This chapter is all about our ONE-ness. By birth we are ONE with Adam. But Jesus calls us to be ONE with *him*. That's the core truth of this section:

We are born ONE with Adam. Be ONE with Jesus.

In the New Testament, Jesus calls himself 'The Bridegroom' (Luke 5:34–35). And the Bible commonly calls his people 'the Bride' (Ephesians 5:21–33). He has all the riches. We have all the debts. And yet, essentially his proposal is this: 'All that I am I give to you, all that I have I share with you.' What's he offering?

Well, to become a Christian involves amazing benefits. We get feelings of purpose, significance and love. We get forgiveness for our sins and a clean conscience. We come in on Jesus' inheritance—heaven and earth, eternal life! That's all great. But the best thing we get from our ONE-ness with Jesus… *is Jesus.*

That's the best thing about marriage, surely. You don't marry someone to get their *stuff.* Hopefully?

You marry them to get *them.* The best thing about ONE-ness with Jesus is we get Jesus. We get to know him. It's personal.

And if we're ONE with Jesus, the Son of God, we get his Father as our Father. We get his Spirit as our Spirit; his brothers and sisters in the church as our brothers and sisters. We come in on the ultimate Royal Family.

John's Gospel puts it like this:

> *To all who did receive [Jesus], to those who believed in his name, he gave the right to become children of God.* **JOHN 1:12**

Let's press into that: If you believe in Jesus—if you trust him—then you receive him into your life. Just like in a marriage where you receive the other person. And to be ONE with the Son of God means entering his family: Together with all his other brothers and sisters, you become a child of the same Heavenly Father, filled by the same Holy Spirit.

So then the question is: Do you want *in* on this?

In one sense, it is very simple to become a Christian. It's as simple as getting married. Saying wedding vows takes a minute or two—but that moment is momentous.

It's like that with Jesus. If you want to be one with him you could say something like:

> *Dear Jesus, I've come to see that you are Lord, and I am not. I'm sorry for my sin and selfishness. Thank you for dying for my sin. Thank you for rising again to give me new life. Please come into my life to take control. Fill me with your Spirit. Walk with me through this life and into your eternity. Amen.*

Words like those aren't magic, they're just the kind of thing you might say if you want to begin life with Jesus. As with wedding vows, the words take a moment to say yet their effects are lifelong. It's therefore important to make sure you understand what's involved. Consider it like marriage prep.

THE SHAPE OF LIFE WITH JESUS

If you become a Christian, it means three things:

A NEW FAMILY

If you are ONE with Jesus, then you become ONE with all the other people who are ONE with Jesus. If you become a child of God, that means you now have a lot of extra brothers and sisters in this big old family called church.

When I say church, I'm not talking about buildings or institutions. I'm talking about a family. Christianity is not a solo-sport—it's a team game where we carry each other through the ups and downs of life. And a relationship with church is indispensable to a relationship with Jesus. The Bible says Jesus and church are as close as a head is to a body (Ephesians 5:21–33).

What happens in church family? Let me highlight a few things. First, at some point you're going to want to get baptised (if you haven't been baptised already). Baptism is like the wedding ring. It's a powerful physical sign of union. Think about it this way: when Jesus got baptised, it declared his ONE-ness with us. When we get baptised it declares our ONE-ness with him.

Another church practice is called the Lord's Supper (or Communion or the Eucharist—there are lots of names for it). It's where Christians eat bread and drink wine together. It's about centring ourselves physically, emotionally, communally—in every way—on the fact that Jesus died for us. You see Jesus' body was torn apart like bread on the cross. His blood was poured out like wine, to give us life. And Communion powerfully proclaims those truths to us.

Crucially, churches also gather around God's word, the Bible. We hear the story of Jesus again to be reminded of his goodness, his wisdom, his victory, his love.

If you're going to be ONE with Jesus, find a church that loves Jesus, loves the Bible and loves one another. You'll need your new family.

A NEW FIGHT

Coming in on Jesus means coming in on a fight. This makes sense when you understand that all of us naturally go the way of Adam. We all go with the flow of a world disconnected from God, and we go with the grain of our in-born selfishness. And Jesus calls us to resist that natural inclination. To fight.

He gives us a new life to live and he gives us his Spirit to help. But we still have our old human nature. We still have the family likeness of Adam. We still struggle with slaveries, with selfishness, with screw-ups. Adam's way clings to me like flesh to my bones even as Christ's Spirit fills me. Which means, I have a battle on my hands.

You may have heard of the phrase, 'The spirit is willing, but the flesh is weak' (Mark 14:38). Jesus said that. It's the way the Bible describes our fight. Even though I have Christ's Spirit, I still have Adam's 'flesh'—his selfish inclinations.

So then, saying Yes to Jesus means saying Yes to a fight—a fight with sin and selfishness. I must go Jesus' way instead. I need to turn consciously from sin and to Jesus.

The Bible calls this change of direction 'repentance'. It's a complete reorientation of your life, and it makes perfect sense. When I married Emma, I didn't just say some vows one Saturday afternoon and then carry on as before. Everything changed. On that day single Glen died and married Glen rose to life. If the marriage is going to work I need, daily, to live as 'Married Glen' and to fight my selfishness. ONE-ness demands repentance. It means I embrace a new fight.

A NEW FRIENDSHIP

In all of this, the point of fighting my selfishness is not because I like a fight. I fight my selfishness because it spoils the enjoyment of my ONE-ness. This ONE-ness with Jesus is an incredibly precious reality. Over 150 times the Bible describes Christians as being 'in Christ'. We're not just *under* his authority, we don't just follow *after* his lead, we're not simply *with* him in solidarity. The Bible says we are *in* him. And you cannot get closer than 'in'!

Here is a relationship closer than a marriage, closer than the deepest human friendship. We have been given intimacy with the God of the universe. And the Christian life is about enjoying that closeness.

We enjoy it through prayer, through worship, through hearing God's word, the Bible, through meditating on its truth, through song, through the friendship of others, through living out Christ's kind of life in the world. All of these can be ways of enjoying this new friendship. Christianity has a profound experiential dimension. We are meant to experience ONE-ness with the God of immeasurable love.

ALL ABOUT LOVE

Love really is the bottom line. As we've moved through the book perhaps you've noticed the theme of love.

- Jesus has given us our vision for *God*. And this God *is* love: a loving union of THREE.

- Jesus has given us our vision of *the world*. And the world is split—there's a TWO-ness to the world. But the God of love gives everything to bridge the divide.

- Jesus has given us our vision for *ourselves*. And he's shown us that we're made for ONE-ness. The meaning of our lives is to know God's love and to pass it on.

So I ask again, do you want in on this—do you want in on *Jesus*? He is offered to you. If you say Yes, there's a new family to enter; there's a new fight to engage; there's a new friendship to experience. But none of that is the price of the Christian life. It's the privilege.

The family, the fight and the friendship are the shape of your ONE-ness with Jesus. And all of it is free—free for the asking. Maybe you could do so using a prayer like the one on page 124. Such a prayer is like a wedding vow. Getting the words right is not the point. ONE-ness is. Beyond the vow there's a life to live and it can start today.

- The THREE invite you in.

- The TWO determine the world.

- Be ONE with the Son of God!

WATCH
'LOVE STORY'

FOR REFLECTION

- How does marriage illustrate what it means to be a Christian?

- 'ONE-ness demands repentance.' How do you react to that statement?

- What are all the challenges and benefits of being ONE with Jesus? How do you feel about the new family, the new fight and the new friendship?

FAQS

FAQS CONTENTS

IS FAITH THE ENEMY OF SCIENCE?

Betty the botanist has been up all night, working in the lab. When Larry, the lab assistant, arrives Betty says, 'Larry, that specimen you gave me yesterday was fascinating. I've been working through the night to run tests on it. I've done a spectral analysis, I've found pharmacological properties that will help us in the fight against Alzheimer's and I've mapped its genome, a first for the species. I can't thank you enough for the specimen.'

'Specimen?' says Larry. 'Yesterday was February the 14th. Valentine's Day? It was a long-stemmed rose, Betty! Do you understand what I gave you?'

So that's the question: Does Betty understand the rose?

From one perspective, she understands it better than anyone else on the planet. From another perspective she's a moron. Because there is more to the rose than can be discovered by cutting it up or putting it under a microscope. And that 'something more' will not be found by doing additional lab work. The meaning of the rose is not the same thing as its material properties. Its meaning will have to be discovered in other ways.

The Christian position is this: the whole world is like that rose. The world is a gift from someone trying to communicate his love—God. It can certainly be studied scientifically, but it can also be understood on other levels because scientific knowledge is not the only kind of knowledge that's possible. And it's not the only kind of knowledge that's desirable. We don't want less than scientific knowledge. But we want a whole lot more.

Betty would be very foolish if she tells Larry, 'This can't be a love gift because that's not written in its DNA.' There is more to the rose than what shows up under a microscope. And there is more to the world than what we discover scientifically.

Science tells us about mechanisms and materials, but it's not set up to tell us about meanings or a Maker. Science is great at asking 'What?' questions and 'How?' questions. But it's not designed to answer 'Why?' questions and 'What for?'

That doesn't mean Christians don't love science. In the 16th and 17th centuries, it was largely Christians who pioneered what we think of in the West as the modern scientific method. They did so at Christian universities for Christian reasons. People like Copernicus and Newton pursued their science because they firmly believed certain truths about God, the world and ourselves.

In fact, the beliefs we've been exploring in this book are foundational to science. To do science you need to believe in three things at least: laws *up above*; a world *out there*; and minds *in here*. And you need to believe that these three things triangulate. You need the laws of nature to rule the world and you need them to be understandable by little old *us*. Albert Einstein thought it was a miracle that these three things lined up. He said: 'The eternal mystery of the world is its comprehensibility... The fact that it is comprehensible is a miracle.'[8] Why should scientific laws hold across time and space and why should they be understood by human beings?

Christian faith casts light on this mystery. It says that God, the world and ourselves are integrated. From page one of the Bible, humans are said to be 'in the image of God' and to have a special role in the world—'naming' and 'ruling' it. We should expect to understand something of the laws *up above* and the world *out there*.

---

8   Quoted in Walter Isaacson, *Einstein: His Life and Universe* (Simon & Schuster UK, 2007), p462.

This Christian faith does not oppose science. Such faith was the soil in which so much of modern science grew. And such faith continues to animate many scientists today. It's not a tug of war between faith and science. When we see a rose we see a botanical specimen *and* a symbol of love. When we see the world we can understand it as a scientist *and* as a person of faith. You don't have to choose.

ISN'T FAITH UNREASONABLE?

PICTURE THIS:

| A leap of faith.

What are you imagining?

Here's how it's usually understood. We reckon that reasonable people live down on ground level. Reasonable people don't leap, they go by logic and evidence. But there are these other people called 'believers' who lose touch with grounded truth, professing to know things which they cannot possibly know. And so, on this understanding, believers are leaping in the air with no foundation, while rational people are grounded, living by logic and evidence.

It's a familiar picture. It's also false. Everyone lives by faith, every day. You have to. You cannot get through the day living purely by what you can deduce logically or prove scientifically. We trust the world as it's presented to us—largely!—and most of what we trust cannot be demonstrated under laboratory conditions.

Every minute we rely on people, on reports, on information and on instructions. I trust the signs to the train station. I trust the guy behind me on the platform not to push me onto the tracks. I trust the driver. I trust that the train and the tracks have been properly maintained. I trust that you'll meet me at the next station the way you promised. Minute by minute we exercise trust that people will be truthful, faithful, law-abiding, ethical, abiding by health and safety, and so on. We have no time or ability to keep checking these things, we have to take it on faith. And above the people we trust there are the principles we value. We believe in human rights, human equality, human dignity, the sanctity of life. You can't prove any of these. But we live on the basis of them. We believe ardently in such values.

Millions of people on planet earth think they are *not* people of faith and yet they believe it's better to give than receive, that a society should be judged by how it treats its weakest members, that you should be free, that people are not property, that you should never sell yourself into slavery, that you should not discriminate against people, especially minorities, that it's better to choose people over things, relationships over money, love over power, kindness over status, humility over pride.

But none of these beliefs are the result of a rational argument. There's no logical proof that concludes: therefore you should love people. You might come across a scientific study that reports 'People who love others live on average eight months longer'. But *that is not the reason you believe in love*. In fact, if that scientific study *is* the reason you believe in love, then you don't really believe in love (and you may just be a sociopath!).

But I'm assuming that you do believe in love. And that actually you probably prize that belief more than the truths you've arrived at by science and reason.

The reality is, none of us live life purely according to logic and evidence. All of us are mid-air, living by beliefs that we hold more precious than anything else. I can't *prove* that all people are equal but I know it more profoundly than any scientific truth. I can't *prove* that love is the greatest power in the world but I know it in a way that goes deeper than logical argument. And if you know these things too, then you are a believer. Welcome to the club.

And here's where *Christian* faith comes in. Christian faith does not tell you to 'leap' up to things you can't know. Instead, consider this: You are already a person of faith. You're already mid-air. That's good. That's fine. That's inevitable. But you need ground beneath your feet. You do need reasons for your faith. And science and logic don't cut it. If we're a cosmic accident, it doesn't make sense to prize humility and sacrifice. If we're a biological survival machine, it makes no sense to believe in human equality. If we are matter in motion, love simply isn't the greatest power.

But if God is love, if he made a world to love and if you are made to share in this love—then there is ground beneath your feet. You have an account of reality that makes sense of your beliefs. Your faith in equality, sacrifice and humility makes sense. Christianity does not add to the absurdity of your world. It uniquely accounts for the values you hold—values that would be absurd if Christianity wasn't true.

Don't leap. Recognise you're already mid-air. Now ask whether Jesus provides the grounding you seek.

IS CHRISTIANITY TRUE, OR JUST WISHFUL THINKING?

PICTURE THIS:

> You approach a fork in the road with no idea which direction to travel. On each path you see a guide. One guide is alive, the other is dead. Which path do you take?

Christianity does not proclaim a dead teacher but a living Lord, and that makes all the difference. The wonderful vision for life we have explored in this book has consoled billions over two millennia. It tells us the world has come from eternal love (see THREE), been redeemed by sacrificial love (see TWO) and is destined for deathless love (see ONE). This is an unequalled vision for life. But is any of it true?

For Christians, that turns on the question of whether Jesus rose from the dead. If he didn't, then death got the better of Jesus and, along with him, it buried all that fine-sounding teaching about love and hope.

But if Jesus beat death, then he (and not death) is Lord. That's the Christian position. Can we believe it today? Let me offer you some reasons to believe that Jesus rose from the dead vindicating his vision for life.

THE HEAVENS

The universe is already preaching to us about life-from-the-dead. Here are some suggestive pointers that show up even in the secular story of our world:

- *Everything has come from nothing.* Out of the void has come life. Reality itself is like Easter: it's all life-from-the-dead.

- *Order has come from chaos.* If humans were going to exist at all, the universe had to be incredibly finely tuned for life. This fine-tuning very much looks like the result of a decision for life over death.

- *Life has come from non-life.* Even from a purely biological point of view, life has come from non-life—which again sounds a lot like Easter. Christians believe that one Sunday a lifeless man rose again. But the secular story says *all* life emerged from non-life (yet without a God of resurrection to work the wonder!).

The heavens seem to be declaring a life-from-the-dead power. And so does history.

HISTORY

THE HISTORY OF THE FIRST CENTURY

The following historical facts can be agreed to by most historians, be they atheists, agnostics, Christians or Jews… Jesus of Nazareth thought of himself as the King of heaven's kingdom, the central figure of history, and the Judge ruling God's future. The Jewish authorities found him guilty of blasphemy and the Romans executed him on account of his claims to kingship. He died on a cross and was placed in a tomb, the whereabouts of which was well known. Three days later, that tomb was empty, and his followers had experiences of the risen Jesus which continued for 40 days and then stopped when Christians say Jesus returned to heaven. The body was never found, and all the eyewitnesses maintained their testimony, even on pain of death.

These are the historical facts, and then the (many) explanations begin. A Christian is someone who considers the alternative theories—Jesus didn't die, his body was stolen, the disciples faked it, or they hallucinated—and judges them to be much less believable than concluding Jesus rose from the dead. It's not that Christians force themselves to believe the most improbable explanation. It's that if you reject the resurrection, you entangle yourself in more absurdity.

HISTORY SINCE THE FIRST CENTURY

The question we should all consider is: Why have we even heard of Jesus? Why didn't Christianity die with Christ on Good Friday, never to rise again? But Christianity didn't remain dead and buried. Far from it. In the words of H.G. Wells:

> *I am an historian, I am not a believer, but I must confess as a historian that this penniless preacher from Nazareth is irrevocably the very centre of history. Jesus Christ is easily the most dominant figure in all history.*[9]

Given he was executed as a rebel and blasphemer in his 30s *and* he's the most famous man who ever lived— an extraordinary resurrection has certainly happened. Somehow Christianity rose from the dead in the first century. Christians say, *Yes, and the explanation is that Christ himself rose.*

Finally, though, to believe that Jesus rose, it must become personal.

HIM

Comic book fans love to debate the relative strengths of their superheroes, thrashing out questions such as, 'Who'd win in a fight between Iron Man and Batman?' Christians do something similar when they consider the ultimate matchup: Jesus versus death. We know

---

9 Quoted in Alister McGrath (ed), *Christian Belief* (Lion Scholar, 2018), p221.

that death has swallowed kings, armies and empires. But we've encountered Jesus in the Bible, and we're persuaded he is Lord.

Whatever it is that brings everything from nothing, order from chaos, life from non-life—whatever that life-giving power might be—Jesus embodies it. And if he really is the cosmic life-giver then of course he conquered death. If he's Lord, the truly remarkable thing would be if he rotted in some Jerusalem tomb.

When a Christian says 'Jesus is Lord', they're not just describing their own personal outlook. They are saying something about the world—that Jesus' vision for life is the true vision, it's how things actually work. We reckon everything—the heavens and all history—find their fulfilment in him.

WHO MADE GOD?

PICTURE THIS:

Billy looks into the night sky in wonder.

'The moon is bright,' he says to his mother. 'How is the moon so bright?'

'The moon is like a mirror,' she replies. 'It reflects the light of the sun.'

Billy is quiet for a moment. 'So the sun shines on the moon and makes it bright?'

'That's right,' says his mother.

Billy thinks a bit more. 'The sun must be *very* bright.'

'It is,' she says. 'Very!'

'So what shines on the sun?'

How would you answer Billy? Surely you'd say something like this:

Nothing shines on the sun. The sun shines all by itself. It's different to everything else in the solar system. Everything else is bright because of the light the sun gives it, but the sun is bright in a different way. It's not bright because of the light of anything else. It's bright because of its own light.

Once you have understood this answer, you've understood how to answer the question, 'Who made God?' The sun is its own source of light and God is his own source of life.

Just as nothing else enlightens the sun, nothing else enlivens God. God is the Source of all life, and has been forever—an eternal Fountain of love. No matter how far back you go, you never get *before* the abundant life and love of God. This is a mind-blowing concept, obviously.

But when we talk about ultimate reality, everyone's view will blow your mind. If we're talking about beginnings, we all need to wrap our heads around something cosmic. There are only three options anyone can take when we think about the origins of all things.

OPTION ONE:

A BEGINNINGLESS UNIVERSE

In this view you could hit rewind on the film of the universe and you would never get to the beginning. Back and back you'd go... 10 billion years... 100 billion years...

1000 billion years… 10,000 billion years… on and on forever the universe is still there. Infinite and eternal. That's an instant-migraine of a thought! The trouble is, most scientists now tell us there *was* a beginning point: a 'Big Bang', let's say. This makes people look for other options, like…

OPTION TWO:

THE UNIVERSE BEGAN, BUT NOTHING BEGAN IT

In this view you hit rewind and, sure enough, you get back before the universe. But at that point there is nothing. Not just a big empty expanse (that would be a whole lot of something). Not just forces and subatomic particles (those are definitely things). What is nothing? The philosopher Aristotle reckoned *nothing is what rocks dream about.* At which point we say, 'But rocks don't dream!' And Aristotle says, 'Exactly! Nothing is *no-thing at all!*'

OK then, but if there was nothing before the universe then nothing turned into everything for no reason. It goes without saying that this view is mind-bending too. To some of us, it's also absurd to the point of impossible. It's usually put forward by people who deny the miraculous. To my mind, though, it's the most miraculous worldview imaginable. With option two *everything* is a miracle— in fact everything is the most improbable miracle of all. And if you share some of my doubts about these first two options, you're left with…

OPTION THREE:

THE UNIVERSE WAS BEGUN BY A BEGINNING–LESS SOMETHING (OR SOMEONE!)

Just like the moon is given light by something that needs no enlightening, the universe is given life by someone who needs no enlivening—an eternal Source of life. As Psalm 90 says: 'Before the mountains were born or you brought forth the whole world, from everlasting to everlasting you are God.' An eternal God—beginningless and endless—is hard to wrap your head around, certainly. But option one seems contrary to evidence and option two seems contrary to logic. It seems to me that option three, however mind-bending, makes the most sense. And it's good news.

According to Christians, the Source of life is not just physics or chemistry, nor is it an infinite nothingness! The Source of all things is an eternal God of love: the Father loving his Son in the joy of the Spirit.

The sun radiates light to the whole solar system—the light of our world. And God radiates life and love to the whole cosmos. The fact that he always has will blow your mind, but—press deeper—if you really get it, this truth will also thrill your heart.

WHY ISN'T GOD MORE OBVIOUS?

PICTURE THIS:

Over dinner one night I tell my children about a screenplay I'm writing.

'Imagine the scene,' I say excitedly. 'It's a spaceship in the future and we begin with a closeup on Sasha. Her eyes spring open as she wakes from deep sleep. She has no memory of how she got there or who she is. She meets two other crew mates on the ship—Hope and Doc. All they know is their names. No one has a clue why they're there. As time goes by they start arguing about the meaning of it all, and then one day a stranger shows up…'

'Wait, wait, wait,' says my daughter. 'It's obvious why they're on the ship.'

'Oh,' I say, deflated. 'Is it? I was hoping it'd be a mystery.'

'There's no mystery,' says my daughter. 'The reason they're there is because you dreamed it all up.' Her eyebrows are merging with her hairline—every fibre communicating: 'Duh!'

'Right, but… Well, first of all, good point.' (I hope a bit of praise will buy me some time. But my son has now sensed weakness. He joins in with his sister.)

'It's obvious, daddy. They're on the spaceship cos it's your story and you wrote it down.'

'Well that's true. On that level, that *is* the reason. But the thing is: none of *them* know that. They don't know me.'

'Daddy!' says my daughter, tapping my forehead. 'Of course they know you. They're all in you. They live in Glen Scrivener's head.' (She enjoys saying my full name. It feels transgressive.)

'Yes! But Glen Scrivener doesn't live in their spaceship.'

'Well maybe he should,' she says, crossing her arms.

'Yeah,' says my son, 'maybe he should!'

Now everyone is frowning.

Have you ever asked the question, 'Where is God?' Some people ask it because of the suffering of the world. Some people ask it because they want to know the presence of God personally. Some people ask it because it seems like an argument against God: surely if he exists he should be obvious.

In a deep sense, though, asking 'Where is God?' is like Sasha asking, 'Where is Glen Scrivener?' And one answer you could give to Sasha is: 'Where *isn't* Glen Scrivener?' Her whole existence is lived in Glen Scrivener's mind. I am inescapable to her. She and everything she knows is a figment of my imagination.

In another sense, Glen Scrivener is foreign to her. He's not a character in the same story—not someone she can interact with on the same level. 'Glen Scrivener' could be written on signs throughout the ship but it wouldn't mean anything to her.

So the author of her life is both inescapable *and* unattainable. It's a fascinating combination and the Bible speaks in similar terms about our relationship with God. In Acts chapter 17 it says, 'in [God] we live and move and have our being'. But at the same time the chapter speaks of our 'ignorance' of God—even though 'he is not far from any one of us'. In one sense we are immersed in the reality of God in every moment and every molecule. In another sense he's on a level that's simply ungraspable.

For Christians, God is not a really powerful supernatural being located somewhere in the universe. That would be like imagining a really powerful space alien in the Sasha story. If I wanted, I could add an intergalactic ruler to the cast of characters in Sasha's story. I could even make him *really* powerful and *really* intelligent. But such an alien would not be the author of the story—only a character alongside Sasha. Likewise, we might imagine that God is a big old Intergalactic Ruler, somewhere out there in the universe (and some people claim to have seen him while others remain unconvinced). But God is not a powerful character in our story, he's the author. God is the author of life: in him we live and move and have our being.

Maybe that makes you feel God's distance, maybe that makes you feel his nearness, but what if I took my children's advice? What if, as I work on Sasha's story, I write Glen Scrivener into it? What if the author becomes a character? Maybe *I* should be the stranger who shows up on the ship. At that point Sasha *could* get to know her creator.

This, of course, is the Christian claim about Jesus. As the Son of the Father, he is our Maker who showed up in history—written into his own story. And this happened in a way *far beyond* the way I could put myself into my writing. In the most profound sense the Author has also become a Character. And just as Sasha might encounter that rescuing Stranger and come to see him as far more, so we can encounter Jesus and find him both greater and more familiar than anything in the world. This Stranger, we come to realise, is our Source. And the God we couldn't grasp becomes the One we can't deny.

IF GOD IS IN CHARGE, HOW CAN I BE FREE?

'I've had enough. I'm leaving this tired old backwater,' says Terry to his friend Belinda. The two goldfish stare out of their tank while the cat dozes on the living room sofa.

'Are you sure?' asks Belinda. 'We're pretty well cared for here.'

'Sheesh, Belinda, they really have got to you, haven't they? This isn't care, it's captivity. Come with me now or regret it forever!'

'Um, I'm good, thanks,' says Belinda.

'Fine,' says Terry, taking one last gulp of water. 'You enjoy your prison cell. I'm gonna breathe free!'

It's a shame that goldfish are so forgetful because, as last words go, these are pretty memorable. 'Breathing free' might be an evocative life goal, but for goldfish it's a death wish. Fish were made for water and they are not freer when they escape the 'confines' of H_2O. Spluttering around on the carpet is not liberation. There is an environment in which fish thrive and there is no freedom worth the name outside that environment.

This is true for humans too. We also have a nature—just like fish, just like everything. And because that's true, there will be environments that lead to an expanded life and those that lead to a diminished life. Freeing ourselves from those life-giving environments is not really freedom. We actually need limits, boundaries and restrictions, and these are not hindrances to true freedom, but helps.

Nowadays those words—limits, boundaries, restrictions—sound oppressive. We commonly think that every limit placed on us is a threat to our freedom. But remember Terry. And remember Jesus too. If you want to see what a truly liberated human being looks like, consider how he walked the earth.

Jesus was clear that he did *not* belong to himself but to his Father. He was on a mission from God and lived to do his Father's will. But that was exactly what made him the free-est man who ever lived. He walked around planet earth with poise and purpose. Secure in the love of his Father, he was undaunted by any and every challenge. And, by the Spirit, he invites us to enjoy this security.

We were made for the love of God. And as with every love relationship it will entail certain limits, boundaries and restrictions. But these are not to inhibit us but to enliven us. We are most free when we are most at home in this life-giving reality.

Our modern view of freedom is usually understood as 'freedom *from*' limits. But Jesus told a series of stories in Luke 15 about 'breaking free' in *that* sense, and it didn't go well. A coin gets loose from its purse, a sheep gets loose from its flock, and a son gets loose from his family. In each case they don't end up free, they end up lost. This is a powerful lesson for modern people to learn. Too often we proclaim ourselves liberated when really we're lost.

And the modern *solution* to feeling lost is also foolish. Modern wisdom says: 'find yourself'. But thirty seconds thought reveals this to be terrible advice. If you are lost, the last thing you need to find is yourself. Because you're lost. And finding a lost person—even yourself—is not that much help. When you're lost, you need to find *home*. And when you're home you can simply *be* yourself. That's freedom.

The good news of Christianity is that Someone has come to us from our ultimate home: from the Father's love. Jesus, the free-est person who's ever lived, can teach us what freedom is. More than that, he can bring us into an experience of this life-giving freedom: a freedom that entails joyful surrender to the most loving embrace.

Goldfish were made for water. We were made for the love of God. When we make our home there, then we are free.

HOW CAN A LOVING GOD JUDGE?

PICTURE THIS:

'That's not kind!' shrieks your daughter as you ban her from screen time.

'Hitting your brother is not kind!' you counter.

'He was annoying me...' she begins.

'That's no excuse. In this house we love each other.'

'Then why are you being so mean?!'

Sometimes people struggle to reconcile a God of love and a God of judgement. Sometimes they imagine that God used to be judge-y (in the Old Testament) but he's chilled out a bit in the New Testament. Some think love and judgement are so opposed that the idea of anything like the biblical God is impossible. But are love and judgement really opposites?

In the scenario above—completely fabricated and unrelated to any happenings in the Scrivener house, obviously—a house of love will mean a house where certain things, like hitting your brother, are ruled out. To have such rules, and to have consequences for breaking them, is loving. It's loving to the brother, it's loving to the household as a place of peace and it's even loving to the daughter. It treats her as a responsible member of the family—someone who is able to love and who is expected to love. It's the same with God.

According to all we've explored in *How to See Life: A Guide in 321*, God is love. He is a fierce and unrelenting Fountain of life and love: a Father loving his Son in the joy of the Holy Spirit. This has been his eternal life and this is what he invites the world to experience. But *because* he is love, his message to the world is: 'In this house we will love each other!' And so his law stands above us as an absolute insistence upon love.

When Jesus summarised the law he said we are to love God with everything we have and we are to love our neighbour even as much as we love ourselves (Mark 12:30–31). This is the good life—a life of love. In fact, it's eternal life. This is how the Son of God has lived forever. Even before the universe began Christ has been loving God, his Father, and loving the Spirit, his neighbour. Now he passes on the good life to us: 'In this house we will love each other.' It's a law of love. And it's a very good thing that our world is under such a 'rule of law'.

We certainly want our *societies* to be based on a rule of law. The alternative is a 'law of the jungle' in which the powerful dominate and the weak are trampled. Without a supreme source of justice above all people and politics, the world would belong to the powerful. Might would trump right. But with God there is a perfect law of fierce, uncompromising love. This is a very good thing.

In the Bible, the analogy of fire is often used of God. He is a consuming fire of love (Song of Songs 8:6) *and* he is a consuming fire of judgement (Hebrews 12:29). These are not in contradiction. The committed, zealous, faithful love of God burns with passion for his beloved and with anger for all that would harm his beloved. In this context the Bible speaks of the wrath of God which is 'his steady, unrelenting, unremitting, uncompromising antagonism to evil in all its forms'.[10] Such fierce anger at evil is not opposed to his love. It is, in fact, the response of love to the evil of the world. If someone was indifferent to the evils of the world we could only conclude that they had a *hard* heart. It's a *tender* heart that is angered by evil. So it is with God. *Because* he is love, *therefore* he judges.

---

10 John Stott, *The Cross of Christ* (InterVarsity Press, 2006), p171.

There are many things we may not know about God's final judgement of the world, but some that we do:

1 *We all deserve condemnation.* We know this because all have violated his laws of love.

2 *We can all be saved.* We know this because Christ has endured a hell of judgement on the cross and risen up to a heaven of blessing—enough for all the world.

3 *We can trust the Judge with the fate of the world.* We know this because Jesus has proved himself on the cross to be perfectly just and perfectly loving.

Something will have the final word on this world. Maybe it's chaos and death, in which case there's no ultimate justice. Maybe it's karma or a distant God, but that holds out little hope for those who know they're guilty.

Christians say, there is good news: we are headed somewhere filled with both justice and love, because the future belongs to Jesus. He has the last word on this world and so we are content to say along with the Bible, 'the Judge of all the earth [will] do right' (Genesis 18:25).

HOW CAN A GOOD GOD ALLOW SUFFERING?

> Once upon a time there was a wise and kind princess ruling over a kingdom of light and everyone was happy, all the time. The end.

As stories go, this is an abject failure. Everyone knows: stories have a shape to them, usually a U-shape. From promising beginnings things fall apart before someone— or perhaps a rag-tag team of plucky misfits—tries to put them back together. Maybe the attempt fails. Maybe it all ends with things worse than ever, but there's always a trajectory. Up or down, there's a shape to a good story.

So here's a far more familiar kind of story. (Any similarities between this story and movies like *Shrek* or *The Super Mario Bros. Movie* are completely intentional!) Picture this:

The kingdom of light is changed forever when a dragon (or a turtle, or a dragon-turtle) swoops in from across the sea. He kidnaps the princess while cowards do nothing. None are brave enough to go after her, except a shepherd from the hills (or an ugly ogre, or an Italian plumber). He's joined by a band of unlikely helpers, who pull together through adversity. They sail through deadly storms, battle terrible beasts, scale impossible cliffs and fight the dragon / turtle / monster to the death. In the end it's the princess who deals the death blow, saving the knight even as he had come to save her. On the voyage home the princess and knight trade insults as the band of helpers roll their eyes. Clearly they are falling for each other. Once home, they marry. The wedding feast lasts for a month and they all live happily ever after. The end.

That's how a story goes. Obviously these characters are ridiculously stereotyped but even if you seek to disrupt conventions, you cannot avoid the necessity for plots to twist, for conflicts to arise and for obstacles to hinder. Sometimes the heroes are more successful, sometimes less so. But all our tales contain struggle, pain and death and the only believable victories over struggle, pain and death are by heroes who go *through* these ordeals.

Every storyteller is a creator of a world. If you have ever told a story, you have been a creator too. And it's almost certain that when you created your world, you allowed struggle and conflict to enter it. You have done what God did to this world. Every creator always does.

Perhaps you object that creating stories is different. After all, in a story no one *actually* suffers, unlike in the world God created. But it's not just about made-up stories. Everything we create involves suffering. If you want to make a business, you know it will be hard. If you want to make art, you know you will struggle. If you want to start a family, you foresee the real suffering that will come—for you and for your children. You do it anyway because life is worth the price of suffering.

But perhaps your objection is that the price is too high. You might concede that *some* suffering is understandable in this world—some bleak chapters make sense in the story— but the *amount* of suffering is just too much. I get that. It's often the way I think, especially when suffering personally or helping others through dark valleys. But here's where I keep returning: the cross.

Ultimately the relationship between God and suffering is seen most clearly in Jesus. He is the God who enters our suffering and experiences it at its fiercest. Anyone who claims that God and suffering cannot coexist needs to spend time contemplating the crucified God. And we need to spend time contemplating what he contemplated. Because, according to the Bible, Jesus made a calculation when he went to the cross: 'he endured the cross' for 'the joy that was set before him' (Hebrews 12:2).

None of us are in a position to make this calculation. *We* can't say whether the suffering of this world is worth it for the sake of some happy ending to come. But Jesus has a unique perspective. He is one who has suffered the world's pain—concentrated down to a single point—and he has seen the future. He *is* in a position to make the calculation. And he thought that his suffering was worth it for the joy that's coming. If even *his* suffering is outweighed by the coming joy, ours certainly will be. A Christian, therefore, depends on Christ's assessment of life, suffering and the future, even in the midst of our pain and confusion. If we trust him we can be assured that there will be no chapter in our story so bleak it cannot be redeemed.

None of this takes away the pain. But it does mean we're given two comforts outstripping anything the world can offer: firstly, the friendship of Jesus in the midst of the trial; and secondly, the future of Jesus beyond it. If he can turn a godforsaken cross into a glorious resurrection, we can trust him to turn our stories—even the story of the whole world—into a cosmic happily ever after.

HOW CAN ANYONE BELIEVE A TEACHING LIKE 'ORIGINAL SIN'?

PICTURE THIS:

'What seems to be the trouble?' asks Dr Jenkins of a wheezing Mr Beale.

'I'm fine, really,' he says between coughing fits, 'I don't know why my wife called you out.'

'Is that your blood?' asks the doctor, pointing to Mr Beale's handkerchief.

'Well… some of it,' he replies. 'A fraction I'd say. Most of it is in my veins.'

'Mr Beale, do you feel pain or pressure in your chest or abdomen?'

'I think you're missing the big picture, Doc. Mostly I feel fine. Yes, there's crushing pain all down my *left* side—pins and needles too—but my right side is perfectly all right, and my eczema from last month has completely cleared up.'

'I'm calling an ambulance.'

'I see you're one of those glass-half-empty doctors,' says a breathless Mr Beale, turning ever more purple. His final words before passing out would become famous in the Beale family: 'I prefer... to focus... on the positives.'

If you're so sick that a doctor has to make a home visit, you don't tell them everything that's *right* with you. You tell a doctor everything that's wrong with you. And your sickness shouldn't keep you from the doctor, your sickness qualifies you for the doctor.

Jesus said, 'It is not the healthy who need a doctor, but those who are ill. I have not come to call the righteous, but sinners' (Mark 2:17).

Jesus is here calling himself a doctor for the spiritually unwell, those born into a sinful condition. He's for sinners. Therefore pretending to be good in the presence of Jesus is like pretending to be healthy while being rushed to hospital. Instead of insisting on all that's right with us, we should own what's wrong.

The Bible calls all of us *spiritually* sick. We are born into a human condition that is distorted and dysfunctional. There are certainly some spiritual Mr Beales in the world, insisting on their own righteousness. But they are self-deceived. The reason the spiritual Doctor has been called is that we're all in trouble. From the very beginning of our lives, every member of the human family shares in the family traits we considered in chapter 5: suspicion, selfishness, slavery, self-justification and screw-ups. In other words, no one has a clean bill of spiritual health.

At this point, many of us object like Mr Beale. 'Mostly I feel fine... My *right* side is perfectly all right.' We point to all the good things about humans in general and about ourselves in particular. And the spiritual Doctor can agree that, yes, there are many things going right in your life. But the hard truth we must all face is that there are *some* things that are not right—and those things are fatal.

Everyone accepts this fact when it comes to our biology. I was born into the world with a certain genetic code, and that code has included a bunch of diseases, disabilities and dysfunctions. More than this, I am genetically predisposed to an even larger range of illnesses and conditions, and between these many ticking time bombs one of them will probably kill me. That's life. And the Bible is simply saying that this is true spiritually as well as physically. It's not that I'm biologically imperfect but spiritually pristine. I am as much of a 'mixed bag' morally as I am health-wise. My health struggles will be differently shaped to yours (maybe I'm predisposed to heart-disease while you're vulnerable to kidney failure). Likewise my moral struggles will be differently shaped to yours (maybe I'm more tempted to pride and you're more tempted to greed). But we all have a faulty condition and we all need the Doctor.

Sometimes this teaching is called 'original sin' but really the emphasis is on *universal* sin—it's everyone's problem. In a very individualised Western culture this often strikes our ears as outrageous because we love the idea that we've *chosen* our identities, rather than been born into them. We tell our stories in terms of what we *choose* to watch or read or listen to, where we *choose* to live, what we *choose* to study, where we *choose* to work, and so on. But actually, I didn't choose where I was born or when. I didn't choose my DNA, my family, my circumstances, my schooling. And those things have shaped me more than any of my individual choices. The older I get, the more I realise—and lament!—*we are all profoundly shaped by our families, sometimes in inescapable ways.*

The Bible encourages us to accept that our story is caught up in a far bigger story (see chapters 5 and 6), and then to offer us a new family (that's chapters 7 and 8). Here we're dealing with that first part: *accepting* how we are shaped by forces beyond our control. And one step towards that acceptance is to realise that there are a thousand things

I didn't choose about myself, but living wisely means responding well to realities greater than me.

Once I accept this, and once I recognise the depths of my sin, it's vital to know that none of this keeps us from Jesus. Our sin qualifies us! In fact *because* we are spiritually sick sinners, the whole world is qualified for the Doctor's care—right from the beginning.

This is a liberating truth. It stops us being spiritual Mr Beales—denying our illness while coughing up blood. 'Original sin' encourages us to get real with the dysfunctions of our lives. If we can own them, there's good news: the Doctor will see you.

WHY CHRISTIANITY AND NOT ANY OTHER FAITH?

PICTURE THIS:

Anderson and Bailey are making their final push to the summit. News comes on the radio: 'Bravo-1-9, avalanche on the southern approach. The fixed lines have been destroyed, over.'

'We need those lines. We'll have to turn back,' says Anderson.

'We can see the summit!' says Bailey. 'Ask about the north face.'

'This time of year?'

'Ask them!'

Anderson sighs. 'Charlie-2-4, what about the northern approach, is that clear? Over.'

'Checking satellite. Stand by.'

Anderson stares down towards basecamp, Bailey at the radio—neither aware of what's incoming from above. After two minutes they hear: 'Bravo-1-9, route clear but once again you would need fixed lines. Advise return to base, over.'

Both know what needs to be done. Neither wants to say it—Bailey especially. Just as he draws breath to concede defeat, he's clapped on the shoulder by a spritely New Zealander, whizzing down from above them.

'G'day fellas,' he says on his way past. They watch, stunned, as he continues his descent.

'I saw you from the top,' he yells, 'so I left my fixed lines on the north face. Enjoy the view!'

It's very common to see world religions as different paths up a mountain. The idea is that all of them get you to the top—God, paradise, enlightenment, and so on. It doesn't matter whether you are walking the Eightfold Path of Buddhism or following the Five Pillars of Islam, everyone is headed in roughly the same direction. But let's ask three questions of this picture.

HOW DO WE KNOW?

How do we know that each path reaches the top? What perspective do you need in order to know that each path is summit-bound? Why are we certain that there are no dead-ends? It seems that you'd have to have a satellite view of the whole terrain. Essentially you need a God's-eye perspective if you're going to claim that 'all paths lead to God'. To think all religions are headed to the same place might sound humble, but in fact it's to assume a God-like view, looking down from above. It's not humble. And it's not a good assessment of world religions, either.

WHAT'S AT THE TOP?

We might assume that all religions are saying roughly the same things, but that assumption can only survive if we remain at a distance from world religions. If instead we care to listen to each religion, we come to see some vital differences. Respecting each faith means not trying to force them into the mould of our preconceived ideas. When we try to understand them on their own terms we see profound differences. They don't even agree on what a religion is. Which is fine. But it does mean we shouldn't presume that every path is heading to the same place.

Let's consider four of the major faiths—those that have at least half a billion adherents. These four religions account for about three quarters of the world's population. Let's ask of these four faiths, how they consider the 'God' question:

- In Hinduism, there are many gods, but above them is an impersonal deity, Brahman.

- In Buddhism, most adherents don't believe in God in any conventional sense. The religion functions perfectly well without a conception of God.

- In Islam, Allah is alone, he is not a father and he has no son.

- In Christianity, God is a loving union of THREE, the Father, the Son and the Holy Spirit.

These present very different conceptions of reality. Adherents of these different faiths are pointing themselves in quite different directions. These faiths do not just represent different paths. They are more like different mountains.

HOW DO YOU GET TO THE DESTINATION?

- In Hinduism, you are rewarded or punished according to your karma.

- In Buddhism, again, it's about karma. If you do good, good will come back to you. If you do bad, bad will come back to you.

- In Islam, the good Muslim strives to be rewarded.

- In Christianity, the Son of God comes down to save us.

Here we have one religion that says God comes down into the pit with us to get us out. The others say, in their own ways, that it's up to us to climb. The religions of the world are not all saying the same thing. Not at all. And Jesus is the most glaring point of difference.

Jesus gives us a unique account of what's 'on top' (God), and a unique account of life 'below' (the spiritual journey). He meets us in our depths and brings us, graciously, to his heights—all out of love. The uniqueness of Jesus is sometimes cast as a bitter pill to swallow. After all, Jesus says things like 'No one comes to the Father except through me', and the Bible contains numerous statements such as 'Salvation is found in no one else' (John 14:6; Acts 4:12). But in fact these are straightforward descriptions of the religious landscape. There simply *isn't* a Father to come to in Hinduism, Buddhism or Islam, so you can't get to him there. There simply *isn't* salvation if you deal with karma or Allah so how could it be found there? If you want a God of eternal love, and if you want a freely offered salvation, there is nowhere else to go. At that point, the uniqueness of Jesus is not a restriction, it's a relief.

HOW CAN I BELONG TO A CHURCH WITH ITS HISTORY, HYPOCRISY AND HATE?

PICTURE THIS:

'Oh my days, what's that noise?!' asks Keeley, looking up from her phone.

'It's sweet,' says India, cocking her head at the video.

'Mute it!' says Keeley, then thinks again. She cranes her head around to India's phone. 'What is it, anyway?'

'It's kids. They're all just learning. Most of them don't even own their own instruments, but every year the school plays Beethoven's ninth symphony.'

'Is that Beethoven?' asks Keeley, screwing up her face.

'That's what it says.'

'No offence babes,' says Keeley returning to her phone, 'but Beethoven is rubbish.'

Given the quality of some performances, the Keeleys of this world might well conclude that 'Beethoven is rubbish'. Likewise, given the lives of many Christians and the scandals of Christian history, you might well think that Christianity is corrupt. That's understandable.

The church has done much evil over its long history. And sometimes the cover-ups have been as diabolical as the crimes. But to use a borrowed analogy: Christians have been given the most beautiful song to sing. It's just that, all too often, we've been completely out of tune.[11] I want to suggest something simple: perhaps the problem is the singers not the song. And perhaps the reason we are *so* heartbroken over the failures of the church is because we know it's meant to be so much better.

Shamefully, we could consider a thousand different scandals in the church, but let me address two—a historic case and a modern one. In considering the crusades and sexual abuse in the church, hopefully you can see how Christians process these evils. Essentially we do two things: we repent of the performance and we return to the song.

---

11 See John Dickson's excellent book, *Bullies and Saints* (Harper Collins, 2021), p23. His third chapter is entitled 'The Beautiful Tune'.

THE CRUSADES

Between the 11th and 13th centuries, armies of Christian soldiers marched under the sign of the cross and killed in the name of Jesus. While much popular misinformation about the crusades abounds and while there is a time and a place to 'bust the myths' concerning these wars, nothing can alter the fact that this is one of many serious moral stains in the history of the church. It's an outrageous performance by those meant to be carrying Jesus' song.

But we should also press into *why* it's so outrageous. Plenty of armies have fought under different banners and killed for different causes (and many of those death tolls have been *far* higher). But we are struck by the evil of the crusaders because they claimed to be singing Jesus' song. The cross is a sign of sacrificial love. Jesus said 'put away your sword', preferring not to overpower his enemies but to die *for* them. We can judge the crusaders precisely because of the song they were meant to be singing.

CHILD SEXUAL ABUSE IN THE CHURCH

Countless scandals have engulfed all nations and denominations such that 'church' and 'abuse' are often readily associated. And it doesn't matter if other institutions have equivalent or worse records, the church is meant to be a refuge: a place both sacred and safe. When people are used and abused—especially children and the vulnerable—that violation of trust is an egregious betrayal.

Once again the response of Christians to such scandals should never be minimisation, cover-up or distraction. We should press into the evils here and own them. We must repent of our 'performance'. And, at the same time, we should return to our song. Because what is it that makes abuse such an evil? The song we're meant to be singing is one in which:

- The vulnerable should be protected;

- The powerful should serve;

- Bodies are like temples;

- Sex is sacred;

- And, as Jesus said,

  'If anyone causes one of these little ones—those who believe in me—to stumble, it would be better for them to have a large millstone hung round their neck and to be drowned in the depths of the sea.' **MATTHEW 18:6**

It's the goodness of Jesus' song which stands above and judges the evil of the church's performance. No wonder that it's *church* abuse that strikes us as so wicked.

How should we then respond? We should be aware that evil, abuse and hypocrisy is not simply a *Christian* problem, it's a *human* problem. We won't escape these evils by avoiding the church, that would only distance us from the song we're meant to be singing. Because actually there are faithful singers today—not pitch perfect but tuneful enough. Their churches seek to repent of bad performances and return to the song, continually.

No one plays Beethoven perfectly. Some do it diabolically. But there are still places you can hear the music—places you can join in. If you're nervous about joining (or rejoining), I understand. You may have to edge your way (back) in. But in spite of its terrible singers, please let the song draw you near.

WHAT ABOUT CHRISTIANITY'S OUTDATED AND BIGOTED VIEWS?

PICTURE THIS:

Belle the Buddhist is over at your place for a barbecue. You offer her a hotdog.

'No thanks,' she says, 'I'm actually vegetarian... It's a religious thing.'

Another guest overhears.

'Oh I get it,' objects Bob the Butcher, mid-burger. '*Meat is murder* and all that, right?! Disgusting!'

Belle is speechless. You lead Bob away by the elbow but he manages to yell a few slurs over his shoulder like 'carnivore-phobe' and 'meat-bigot'.

> Once you get him alone Bob exclaims: 'Unbelievable! The narrow-minded prejudice of some!'
>
> 'I know' you say, trying to find Bob a mirror.

In some ways Christians are like Belle at a barbecue. It didn't used to be the case, but nowadays we hold views that are out of step with majority opinion. We believe in certain things and act in certain ways that are different, and not always popular.

Among Buddhists, some eat meat and some don't, but they are all committed to 'ahimsa' or non-violence— avoiding all unnecessary killing. If you took the time to ask Belle her views she would tell you about a grand vision for life, suffering, karma and the universe. It's a cosmic view of reality that can have some pretty mundane applications—like not having a hotdog. But when Bob the Butcher accuses her of carnivore-phobia he's making a fundamental mistake. He is assessing Belle's behaviour without being curious about her beliefs. And he sees hatred where none exists. If pressed, Belle might well say that 'meat is murder' and Bob might understandably be offended. But none of that means that Belle hates Bob or that she's motivated by bigotry. She sees things differently and she can still love those who disagree. Christians, at our best, hope to be like that.

We have a different vision for life. And, among many other things, two aspects might stand out in the 21st century. Where much of the world has embraced abortion at scale, seeing a million unborn children killed each year, we continue to stand against the killing of our fellow humans. And where the modern West sees sex as something detachable from marriage and family, we continue to see it as something that belongs in the union of one man and one woman for life. When it comes to 'hot button issues' like abortion and sex, Christians are weird.

But then, Christians have long been weird. In the first centuries of the church, Christians were considered extremely odd for saving babies that had been left to die and adopting them instead. (Most cultures have practised some kind of infanticide, especially of girls and the disabled.) Christians have always been different when it comes to babies. We've also always been different regarding sex. In line with the teaching of Jesus, Christians from the beginning have sought to keep sex within marriage (Matthew 19:4–12). And those early Christians did so in cultures where elite men routinely forced themselves on whomever they pleased, whenever they pleased. Christians thought and acted differently and over time, society came to adopt more of that Christian vision.

Fast forward 20 centuries and now, on questions of abortion and sex, Western society has regressed back to ancient practices—that's the way Christians see things, anyway. Nevertheless, we continue to believe that Jesus' vision for God, the world and you is life-giving. That means we are called to be counter-cultural. Unavoidably we will seem like Belle at the barbecue. But if you ask us *why* we take unpopular views, we can tell you about a Jesus-shaped vision for life.

ON ABORTION

Jesus shapes our view. He joined the human race at the point of conception (Luke 1:31). It's not just biology textbooks that tell you 'life begins at conception', Christianity says it too. From conception we have brothers and sisters in the womb. They are very small, very weak and very vulnerable. But Jesus teaches us how to treat people who are small, weak and vulnerable: with all the protection and provision that love demands.

ON SEX

Jesus also shapes our view. As we say in chapter 8, marriage is a picture of Christ's love story. The committed one-ness of marriage reflects the committed one-ness of Jesus with his people. And according to the Bible the physical one-ness of sex belongs in that committed one-ness of marriage. Sex is not just for recreation or for procreation—it's a *proclamation* of a cosmic love story.

There is so much more to say on these issues, but if you look at Christians and are tempted to cry 'bigot' or '-phobe', first look into the reasons why Christians hold such views. You may discover that the differences are motivated, not by hate, but by a grander vision and a deeper love.

WHAT NOW?

IF YOU HAVEN'T ALREADY, HERE'S A REMINDER OF THREE WAYS YOU CAN TAKE THINGS FORWARD.

READ JOHN'S GOSPEL.

Our free 21-day Bible reading plan is available now at YouVersion and Bible.com

EXPERIENCE 321 — THE ACCOMPANYING COURSE.

Watch, listen and learn via our interactive course. Remember to sign in to access the content.

JOIN WITH OTHERS.

Learn together with friends (and/or make new ones) by doing *321* in a group. Find ways of connecting with others, online or in person.

a division of **10** of**those**.com

10Publishing is the publishing house of **10ofThose**.
It is committed to producing quality Christian resources
that are biblical and accessible.

www.10ofthose.com is our online retail arm selling
thousands of quality books at discounted prices.

For information contact: **info@10ofthose.com**
or check out our website: **www.10ofthose.com**